5·23·77

Flowers in Design

. . . for my mother,
whose perennial favorite
is the purple lilac

I LOVE A FLOWER, WHICH ONE I CANNOT TELL

— H. HEINE

Flowers in Design

A Guide for Stitchery and Fabric Crafts

Shirley Marein

A Studio Book · THE VIKING PRESS · New York

Acknowledgments

I wish to express my appreciation and thanks to all the artists
who contributed examples of their work. Special thanks, too, to
those who generously allowed me to photograph their antiques
and collectibles. I was delighted to have the permission of my
lifelong friends Kate and Angel Flores for the poetic translations
used in this book.

My sincere gratitude goes to Barry Seelig for his sensitivity
and delicacy in photographing the lovely examples of flowers.

It has been a pleasure to work once again with Eleanor Bello
on the renderings for the illustrations and with Alan Sweetman
on the photography and the processing of the photographic prints.

Also by Shirley Marein

Off the Loom: Creating with Fibre
Stitchery, Needlepoint, Appliqué and Patchwork:
A Complete Guide
Creating Rugs and Wall Hangings: A Complete Guide

Text and black-and-white photographs Copyright ©
Shirley Marein, 1977. Color photographs copyright in all
countries of the International Copyright Union by Shirley
Marein, 1977. All rights reserved. First published in 1977
by The Viking Press, 625 Madison Avenue, New York,
N.Y. 10022. Published simultaneously in Canada by The
Macmillan Company of Canada Limited.

Library of Congress Cataloging in Publication Data
Marein, Shirley.
    Flowers in design.

    (A Studio book)
    1. Textile crafts.   2.   Embroidery.   3.   Design,
Decorative—Plant forms.   I.   Title.
TT699.M37   746   76-54302
ISBN 0-670-32204-0

Text and black-and-white photographs printed in the
United States of America. Color photographs printed in
Japan.

Acknowledgment is hereby made for permission to re-
print the following: Angel Flores: "Interior of the Rose"
by Rainer Maria Rilke, translated by Kate Flores. Copyright © 1960 by Angel Flores. (From *An Anthology of
German Poetry from Hölderlin to Rilke,* edited by Angel
Flores. Anchor Books, 1960). "The Rose" by Gabriela
Mistral, translated by Kate Flores. Copyright © 1961
by Angel Flores. (From *An Anthology of Spanish
Poetry from Garcilaso to Garcia Lorca,* edited by Angel
Flores. Anchor Books, 1961). Reprinted by permission
of Angel Flores.

Penguin Books Ltd.: "The Fall of the Flowers" by Yen
Yün from *The Penguin Book of Chinese Verse,* translated by Robert Kotewall and Norman L. Smith (1962).
Copyright © Norman L. Smith and Robert Kotewall,
1962. Reprinted by permission of Penguin Books Ltd.

Contents

Preface

Those of us who wonder at the perfect but ephemeral beauty of a flower often have an intense desire to extend and preserve its image—perhaps to awaken again the feeling of warm affection it evoked, for flowers are a source of great delight and the living plant is a lasting pleasure. Shakespeare felt that "beauty within itself should not be wasted." In *Venus and Adonis* he observed:

> *Fair flowers that are not gath'red in their prime*
> *Rot and consume themselves in little time.*

For some the best way to preserve a strong emotional sentiment may be in a poem or a song; for others it may be in an oil painting or a fresh watercolor. Another traditional expression of love and affection may well be a birthday cake with pink and white petals forming a sugary embrace. But many of the world's most beautiful floral designs have been created by craftsmen who work with thread and fiber.

The flower in art and design is an integral part of the history of art. With few exceptions, in the arts of all cultures the flower is a recognizable presence, assuming either a major or a minor role. Occasionally adaptations from other periods and other cultures obscure its orderly progression through art history. Beautiful fabrics, ceramics, trinkets, painting, and sculpture have been acquired by travelers and conquerors since the beginning of time. The Romans were well-known collectors of luxury items as well as of antiquities. All through history artists and craftsmen have migrated, traveled, have been sent to study, or were impressed into service, in foreign countries. By adapting and building on new ideas, the artist implemented the assimilation of design elements. Gentile Bellini, a Venetian painter of the Renaissance period, for example, was summoned to Constantinople to serve the Islamic sultan. Whether or not the Renaissance artist had any effect on Turkish art is questionable, but Islamic design did affect Renaissance design. Changes in the past were gradual; it was not until the twentieth century, after such events as the Paris International Exposition of 1925, that the design ideas of the entire world became quickly available to us for study, for adaptation, for revival.

Representation of the deity Horus as the rising sun on the lotus flower. From an Egyptian painting.

OPPOSITE: *Still Life, Flowers.* Henri Matisse (1869–1954). Collection Dr. and Mrs. Frederick Mebel.

Grecian lotus designs.

Detail of a fifth-century B.C. Greek volute. Museum of Fine Arts, Boston. H. L. Pierce Fund.

Flower design may be copied directly from nature. The eye sees a photographic image, which we know can be accurately reproduced by the camera. For the artist, it is important that the image seen, when it is transmitted by the eye to the brain and thence to the hand, will in turn communicate a very personal individual expression. Henri Matisse described his line drawings as the most direct and purest translation of his own emotions. But flower designs can also be worked out geometrically, using mathematical divisions and a compass to produce images with the stately precision of a rosette on a Greek volute. Although there is no substitute for firsthand observation of fresh flowers and growing plants, designers of floral fabrics and wallpaper keep at their fingertips a graphic file of reference material drawn from historical sources, photographic examples, seed catalogues, and contemporary paintings.

It is intended that the examples presented in this book will serve not only as references but as inspiration, or just plain enjoyment for all who love flowers in design.

An early reference to flowers is the description in the Bible of those in the Garden of Eden. Although such a garden would have been a tangle of wildflowers, at the very least we must accept with faith the presence of apple blossoms (unless we go along with the heresy of those researchers who feel the famous apple could have been an apricot). Carvings and painted patterns within Egyptian tombs, more than three thousand years old, depict recognizable but highly stylized flowers. Ancient Sumerians and Egyptians decorated their homes with plants grown in containers in much the same way they are grown today. And the Hanging Gardens of Babylon were one of the Seven Wonders of the ancient world.

With the possible exception of certain desert and Antarctic areas, the world is full of flowers; more than 350,000 known specimens are recorded. These include the rarest of species, the commonest of weeds, the most minute of wildflowers, and the largest of tropical exotica; and most remarkable, the hybrid, a result of human endeavor.

There are some flowers so delectable that they are felt to be as savory as they are beautiful. Consider the rare rose-petal preserve, for instance, the delicacy of filled squash blossoms, or heady dandelion wine. Food editors have rightly extolled the wonders of the vanilla bean, often unaware that it is the fruit of an orchid. And how sweetly satisfying it is to know that the tasty *fraise des bois*, the wild strawberry, is in truth a pollinated flower of the rose family.

And then there are the flowers thought to cure almost any ailment. Before modern medicine the members of the mallow family (and it is indeed a large family of about two hundred relatives, including hollyhocks, hibiscus, the cotton plant, rose of Sharon, and the okra plant) were known to cure everything from chapped hands, bruises, baldness, bee stings, dandruff, colds and sore throats to constipation. The sticky marshmallow was one of the finest sources of medicinal balm known to the Puritans. Boiled in sugar, then cut into chunks, the marshmallow root also provided a very popular confection.

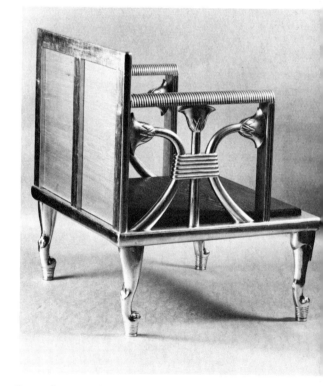

Reproduction of a chair from the tomb of Queen Hetepheres I, with stylized papyrus flowers in the side arms. Museum of Fine Arts, Boston.

9

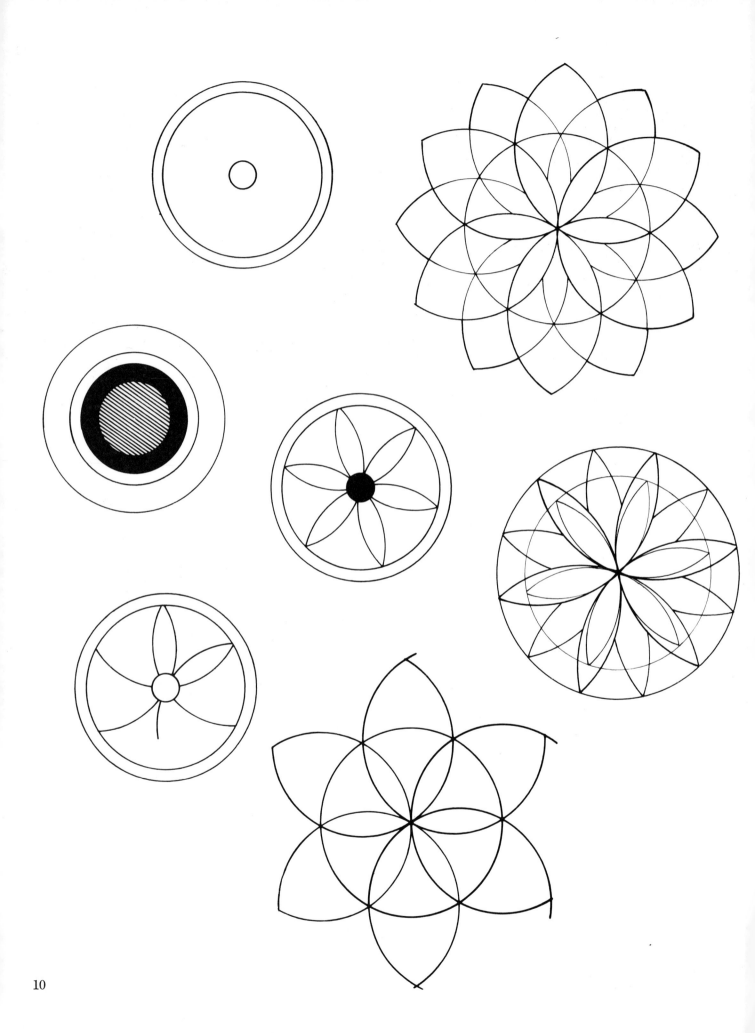

Making flower forms with a compass.

11

To see a World in a Grain of Sand
And a Heaven in a Wild Flower.

—William Blake,
Auguries of Innocence

The Origin and Cultivation of Flowers

Many of our choicest fruits and flowers originated in Asia, evolving through experimentation in well-established countries with advanced civilizations. It is necessary to link fruits and flowers together because all flowering plants bear fruit and many belong to the same family groups as those bearing edible fruit. Most orchard fruits—the apple and the pear, the plum, cherry, and peach—belong to the Rosaceae or rose family. Apples as we know them today are descended from small, thin trees with spiny branches that flourished in Asia and in some European woodlands. These wild species produced pink and white blossoms and tiny fruit. The Roman naturalist Pliny, during the first century A.D., recorded twenty-two known varieties of apple, many the result of grafting.

Seeds, plants, and agricultural technology were brought to the West by merchants and travelers following the China trade routes through India, Persia, and Turkey. We are indeed indebted to the Chinese for the development of many of our favorite garden flowers, particularly peonies, camellias, gardenias, chrysanthemums, and most probably roses as well. Their early efforts at selection, cross-breeding, and hybridization were no doubt intended to improve plants used as food, for medicinal purposes, and as items of trade, and not just for their beauty.

In the Far East the lotus was cultivated for food, as were the tubers of lilies and the bulbs of tulips. Flowers and plants were used to make a variety of perfumed and flavored teas. The tea plant, if left unpruned, bears white flowers shaped like the camellia, a member of the Theaceae or tea family of plants. Oil from pressed flowers provided the base for perfumes, as highly valuable an export commodity in ancient times as it is today. Almost beyond comprehension is the reality of pressing one ton of damask rose petals in order to distill one pound of rose oil or attar of roses. Entire valleys have been devoted to the production of beautiful flowers containing parts and substances used for many purposes. Another plant of great value is the infamous *Papaver somniferum*, source of both innocent poppy-seed topping and the dangerous drug opium.

Strange how many flowers have names of Greek origin—the amaryllis, the chrysanthemum, and the alyssum, for instance—and yet there was very little formal gardening in ancient Greece, although there were many native wildflowers. Small

Poppy. Photograph by Barry Seelig.

OPPOSITE: *Chrysanthemum.* Piet Mondrian (1872–1944). The Solomon R. Guggenheim Museum, New York.

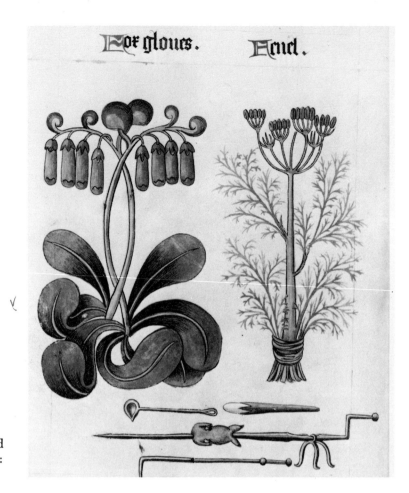

Plates from the sixteenth-century portfolio acquired by Elias Ashmole. Below: Lily and lavender. Right: Foxglove and fennel. © Bodleian Library, Oxford.

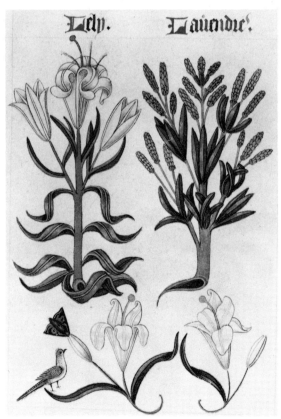

bulbs, seeds, and shrubs grown in the humidity of bell jars were used on special occasions and for celebrations. The Greeks might have engaged in more elaborate horticulture had they been less interested in the arts, architecture, and philosophy. However, Theophrastus in the fourth century B.C. did describe and classify about 450 plants in his *History of Plants*. The more gregarious Romans, more given to luxurious extravagance, literally slept on beds of roses. Egypt supplied Rome with barges of fresh flowers. It is said that Cleopatra at a dinner given for Mark Antony had the floor covered with rose petals to a depth of eighteen inches. The demand for fresh roses was so great that the Romans devised a method for piping vapor heat into hothouses with windows made of mica, in order to force roses into bloom.

Parts of Africa, such as the huge Sahara wasteland and the dry, windswept plains with their great variations in temperature, are rather poor in flowering plants. For the most part, before the expansion of the Roman Empire and the return of the Crusaders from the East, Europe too had decidedly less spectacular species than those found in warmer climates. The greatest number of flowering plants is probably found in the tropics of South America, particularly the Amazon basin. Ground untilled for centuries in sparsely populated primitive areas, undisturbed vegetation, and humid rain forests produce flamboyant climbers

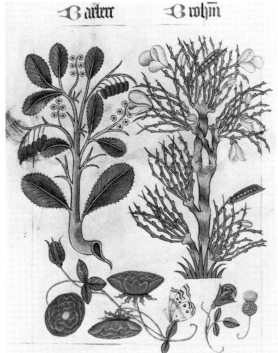

Hellebore and fleur-de-lis (left) and barberry and broom (below) are also among the plates in the Ashmole portfolio. © Bodleian Library, Oxford.

and plants that reach maturity and reproduce themselves more rapidly than elsewhere. However, the great coniferous and deciduous forests of North America and Western Europe contained many thousands of plants too. Most of these are wildflowers, but wildflowers, like jewels, are often hard to find. Sometimes undetected, these precious miniatures, alone or in groups of friendly clusters, sparkle in dappled forests, sunny clearings, or melting snow, enjoying their greatest glory in the spring.

Much of the legendary lore about flowers and plants contains a great deal of fancy in addition to fact. Imagine the reverence accorded to flowers believed to have restorative or magical powers, or the ultimate power of death. In myth and in history, Medea, Cleopatra, and Lucretia Borgia are portrayed as willful mistresses of many lethal brews. And yet many of the same flowers and herbal essences used as poisons, when judiciously administered, were curative. The medicinal properties of foxglove, for instance, were known to the ancient Greeks and Romans. In medieval times the plant was grown intentionally as a magic potion because it could kill undetected. Much later digitalin was recognized as a drug for slowing and strengthening the heartbeat and was extracted from foxglove seeds. Poultices of crushed flowering plants, often combined with fats, were used to treat a great variety of ailments in the early days of medicine

Pansy embroidered in silver-gilt and silk thread on satin. Late sixteenth century. Victoria and Albert Museum, London.

Vine border on a fragment of Coptic fabric of the fourth or fifth century. Author's collection.

OPPOSITE: Daffodils worked in tent stitch on cloth appliquéd to a background fabric, 1600. Victoria and Albert Museum, London.

and were quite successful because so many bruises, aches, and pains responded to soothing emollients—and others eventually cure themselves anyway.

During the early Middle Ages, when the accumulated knowledge of classical antiquity appeared to be lost, European monks kept alive the knowledge of plants, fruits, vegetables, and healing herbs within monastery walls. They recorded information, kept well-tended gardens, and shared seeds and cuttings with the local people. In the twelfth and thirteenth centuries, during the Age of Chivalry, the planned flower garden was a romantic oasis that grew and developed through the Renaissance into the excessive extravagance of the Baroque period. Gardening as an art form reached its ultimate formal expression in the elegance at the French palace of Versailles. During the reign of Louis XIV, the brilliant landscape architect, André Le Nôtre, expanded the concept of vast formal gardens and spacious public parks with extensive vistas. Orangeries were the elaborate greenhouses of the seventeenth and eighteenth centuries. Warmed by charcoal braziers, they supported thousands of orange trees growing in tubs, as well as figs, pomegranates, and palm trees.

Le Nôtre's principles of formal design dominated Europe until the natural gardens of the English countryside became increasingly popular. The craze for indoor gardening and floral decoration in the ordinary household began in the days of Queen Victoria. The nurturing of tropical plants started as a status-seeking fad among middle-class Victorians in search of the exotic for their overdecorated but sacrosanct parlors.

Warmed by the Gulf Stream, the Atlantic coast of Great Britain is mild enough to support the cultivation of many flowers and herbaceous plants native to warmer regions of Asia and to countries bordering the Mediterranean. The English countryside is famed for the beauty of its wild primroses, violets, and bluebells. Because of travel and exchanges between the East and Europe, in Elizabethan England—Shakespeare's England— native plants from the East and the southern areas of Europe were already well established and recorded in literature and art. Collector Elias Ashmole acquired, in the seventeenth century, a portfolio of drawings on vellum of English flowering plants, trees, and shrubs. This collection of plates, now in the Bodleian Library at Oxford University, is thought to have been drawn by an artist living sometime between 1520 and 1530 as a source book of floral detail or a pattern book for others in the applied arts. In addition to plants native to the British Isles, these drawings reveal pomegranates, almond, olive, and mulberry trees, the plum and the peach, lavender, lilies, the garden pea, and England's national flower, the rose. One of the oldest plants in the world, well known in Egypt five thousand years before Christ, flax, the source of linseed and linen fiber, was also cultivated.

The northeast coastal Indians of America used clam shells for hoes and dug with stone implements; their cultivated crops were rather limited. A great many native plants were harvested without cultivation, including berries of all kinds, maple sugar, leaves for brewing beverages, flowers and roots for dye, bayberry wax for candles, and fibrous plants for weaving baskets. The

bark and leaves of the native flowering dogwood were used for smoking and the roots for dye. Corn and beans were cultivated in mounds. Sunflowers, squash, and pumpkins were planted between the rows. These staples were augmented by the cultivation of the tobacco plant and of gourds for containers and dishes.

Settlers coming to North America brought many seeds with them, hoping to make the transition comfortable and more familiar. They planted their seeds to produce vegetables and medicine; flax seeds for the cultivation of linen fibers, and possibly some seeds for flowers.

Later, seeds and bulbs for hollyhocks, foxglove, pansies, primroses, tulips, pinks, marigolds, and daffodils could be obtained from nurseries, but they were rare; it is likely that homesteaders exchanged them with one another. Today's garden standbys—geraniums and petunias, peonies and chrysanthemums—were unknown.

Just what is a cultivated flower? The outward appearance of the flower, of the thousands of varieties, is astonishing in its diversity, and yet the inner parts are similar, concerned with fruit and seed. The beautiful petals and protective sepals are coverings for the inner reproductive system, the pistil and the surrounding stamens. The pistil consists of three parts; a round hollow at the base contains the ovary with its inner chamber of minute ovules supporting a slender stem or column. The sticky-surfaced stigma crowns the top of the style. Each stamen is a slender stalk holding an anther at the top where pollen forms.

Brass bells cast in the form of a Canterbury bell (above) and a madonna lily (right). Collection Benine Adolf.

When the anthers open and a wind-wafted grain of pollen becomes attached to a stigma, it sends out a slender thread carrying a single cell down through the style to unite with one in the ovule.

Flowers, like people, owe their appearance to characteristics inherited through the union of cells. In a moist woodland or meadow, common blue violets always present a most familiar appearance, with nodding heads and purplish-blue petals, their white centers extending outward with a delicate fuzz on the lower side petals. Each rounded heart-shaped leaf provides a handsome background for the sweet-smelling flowers. Occasionally one will find white-petaled violets having fine blue veins and leaves of the same shape as the common blue violet. These are not true white violets, but the result of a chance happening in pollination, a rearrangement of genes that has caused the seedling to differ from its parent. In some flowers the petals may be a different color; in others they might be tinged with two colors, possibly have double petals, fringed petals, or grow very large.

In the controlled environment of the garden or nursery, these new forms can easily be recognized. If the new plants are desirable, they are separated from the parent group. With care the new strain may be propagated from cuttings or purposefully bred. Most garden flowers have been developed through selection, crossbreeding within a species, or hybridizing by crossbreeding different species. The appearance of new plant forms often initiates new designs.

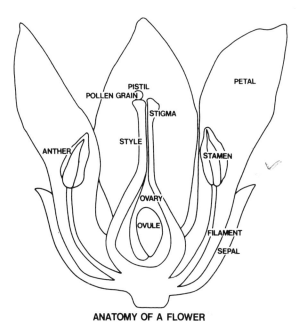

ANATOMY OF A FLOWER

Anatomy of a Flower. Needlepoint on canvas by Shirley Marein, 1975, and (above) a diagram of the same subject.

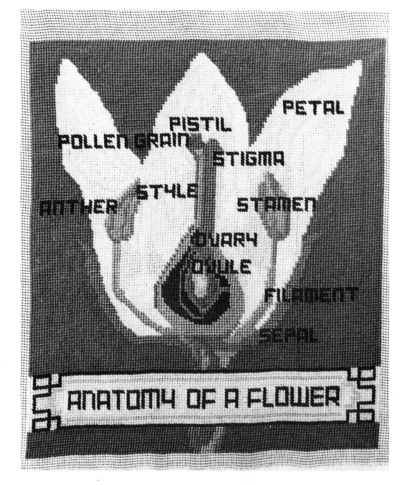

The Fall of the Flowers

The splendour of Spring slowly, slowly departs—but
    whither?
Once more I face the flowers, and raise my cup.
All day I ask of the flowers, but the flowers make no
    reply:
For whom do you fade and fall?
For whom do you blossom?

                                    Yen Yün

The Lyrical Approach

The lotus, Buddhist symbol of one of the eight precious things, an emblem of happy prophecy, and a symbol of divine purity and pledge of Nirvana.

The Chinese began the cultivation of the chrysanthemum about 500 B.C., just about the time they were replacing their stone hoes and wooden digging sticks with cast-iron hoes and plowshares. Ancient Chinese tradition set a high standard for craftsmanship, aesthetic appreciation, and accomplishment in the arts, and developing both the chrysanthemum and the peony became an exacting art form.

At an even earlier time calligraphic writing, the ultimate accomplishment in the practice of an exacting art form, had already influenced many other forms of Chinese art. Because their calligraphy, drawing, and painting are so similar, basically employing the same materials, there is a definite tendency to reflect the same feeling for linear design. Nature is expressed in sensitively balanced compositions dominated by a lyrically flowing line.

Literate Chinese gentlemen spent years training hand and eye in the skillful manipulation of the brush. Such perfection was extremely important during the Shang Dynasty when people believed they could communicate with their ancestors only through writing, rather than through speech and prayer. The nature of the materials—the use of ink on paper or silk—meant that the artist had to be so intimately acquainted with the essence of his subject that he could express it freely and spontaneously. There was no opportunity to rework and restructure his ideas, to erase and revise. Each brushstroke was the direct expression of a fully formed conception, and the result was the rhythmic vitality that characterizes Chinese art.

Culture of the silkworm and the weaving of silk fabric had begun in China long before the Shang Dynasty (1766–1122 B.C.). Legend has it that in 2640 B.C. the wife of the Emperor Huang Ti encouraged the growth and feeding of silkworms and the development of the process of reeling the silk from the cocoons. Sericulture remained a well-guarded secret in China for more than three thousand years. The monopoly laid the foundation for China's wealth.

Many of the paintings surviving from this period are drawn on fine silk and contain written poems. Other silk fabrics woven at this time have for the most part disappeared. The drawloom,

Symbols of two of the Eight Taoist Immortals, the lotus of the patroness of housewives (above), and the flower basket of the patron of gardeners and florists.

OPPOSITE: Chinese k'o-ssu tapestry medallion. Museum of Fine Arts, Boston.

21

Representations of the lotus and the peony in cut-velvet fabric. The fylfot (or swastika) cross is a common decorative motif in many cultures.

Peonies and viburnum in a fragment of Chinese k'o-ssu silk tapestry of the Southern Sung period, 1127–1279. © British Museum, London.

with its mutiple heddles hand-lifted by a man known as a drawboy, is believed to have originated in China. Its invention made possible many fundamental weaves, such as twill, damask, and satin. Judging from the sophistication of technique, tapestry, which was known as *k'o-ssu* to the Chinese, also dates from a very early period. The word *k'o-ssu* literally means broken thread, referring to the method of stopping or interrupting the weft thread in order to change colors. The technique is the same as that used in weaving Gobelin tapestry, which also shows open slits in the weave as a result of the method of making color changes, except that both warp and weft were woven entirely of silk. Gobelin tapestry during its periods of greatest excellence had slits of about three-quarters of an inch, whereas in Chinese silk tapestry the slits measure about an eighth of an inch. A large silk tapestry sometimes took between fifteen and twenty years to complete.

A wide range of colors and the delicacy of silk fiber made it possible to represent in tapestry, with great precision, the well-rounded, gently curving forms of such things as flowers and birds. After the weaving was completed, details were strengthened and defined by the artist with paint and paintbrush. Although this is an expedient afterthought much frowned upon by purists, it seems of little consequence because of the close relationship between the art of tapestry and the art of painting during this period. In ancient China (and today in Japan) the creative talents of all artists were revered. The arts were encouraged and patronized by the court. Even today the famous weavers of that time are known by name. As tapestry was con-

Floral cut-velvet border. Chinese.

Late sixteenth-century Ming brocade with lotus blossoms. Museum of Fine Arts, Boston.

Chinese embroidery on black silk with brocade border. Collection Theda Sadock.

OPPOSITE: Detail of a k'o-ssu tapestry panel. Museum of Fine Arts, Boston.

sidered a precious fabric, it was used to decorate official clothing, in decorative panels, and as a cover for books. Tapestries featured birds, both naturalistic and mythological, and small animals and flowers. Peacocks, ducks, and geese were usually portrayed against a floral background of peonies and of flowers composed of multiple florets. Gold and silver thread enhanced a wide range of richly colored silk fibers.

Designs by the remarkable painters and weavers of the Sung Dynasty, a period extending from the tenth to the thirteenth century A.D., are broad in concept and appear as contemporary as some of today's graphics. Line is as much a prime concern in their well-balanced compositions as it was centuries earlier. It is used to delineate and enclose forms. Modeling of form in light and shade, and perspective and color are secondary, and when they were introduced they reflected Western influences. Pictured images were drawn in fine black-ink brush line, with flat washes of color filling the interior areas. Representation of human beings, demons, animals, flowers, and plants were set off from the background by these black outlines. Often surrounded by space, the individual outlined image tended to have more importance.

To many, the flattened images isolated from each other have the effect of an abstract conception. Rarely did the early Chinese artist paint from life. He observed and then recorded objectively without emotionally intruding upon the subject. Even people

Contemporary Japanese ginger jar with cherry-blossom design.

OPPOSITE LEFT: Panel from a Chinese costume. Embroidery on celadon-colored silk. Author's collection.

OPPOSITE RIGHT: Chinese floral braid buttonhole closure with silk brocade. Author's collection.

Blue-and-white-ware jar with lion-head handles and floral decoration, Yuan Dynasty, fourteenth century. The Cleveland Museum of Art. Purchase, John L. Severance Fund.

pursuing their daily activities were portrayed as apparently unaware of being observed. Flowers, birds, entire landscapes appear to exist in a timeless arrangement, remote from human intervention. These designs are true to form and color but without photographic fidelity. Clarity, assurance, and a sense of perfection are achieved through close observation of nature.

The glories of the Chinese fiber artists were their incredible compound weaves, tissue-thin silk fabrics, velvets, and tapestry-woven textiles. Embroidery most certainly was of secondary importance, functioning as a further embellishment. But then again when these magnificent fabrics were embroidered with fine silk, gold, and silver threads, they often surpassed Byzantine and medieval ecclesiastic vestments. Blinding perfection was achieved with a limited number of stitches. Satin, chain, long and short stitches, and small knots predominated, with the addition of couching and laidwork for the gold and silver threads. Imperial robes were embroidered with sacred symbols. Many images were limited to the use of the Emperor and Empress. The dragon, for instance, represented God, nature, and the Emperor, and personified all the powers of heaven and earth, the entire mystery of the universe. The surrounding floral designs symbolized the four seasons: peonies and peach blossoms for spring, the lotus flower for summer, the chrysanthemum for autumn, and the sacred lily (of the narcissus family) for winter. On

secular clothing each separate and distinct design also had meaning and recognizable significance. Many of the symbolic meanings in Chinese design were founded in the philosophical teachings of Confucius and Lao-tzu.

The lotus flower inspired all craftsmen because it signified purity, immortality, and rebirth. It can be found on pilasters, at the base of sculpture, as a porcelain vase form, in painting, on textiles, and in embroidery. The pomegranate and the fish, because they produce many seeds and eggs, represented fertility. The natural design possibilities inherent in the many varieties of butterflies were utilized to the fullest by Chinese designers to express happiness.

All existing examples of Chinese carpets are of rather recent origin. The earliest known examples are from the Ming period, fourteenth to the seventeenth century A.D. on through the reign of the Emperor Ch'ien L'ung (1735–1796) when the finest

Japanese fan print of morning glories. Hiroshige.
Museum of Fine Arts, Boston. Spaulding Fund.

Flower motifs in Japanese family crests.

carpets, many rich in floral design, were produced. Carpets may have been in use as interior furnishings at an even earlier time in China proper. As far as is known, the very earliest (approximately fifth century A.D.) knotted carpet was found in the Pazryck valley near the Altai mountain region of Mongolia, but its over-all appearance and individual designs are characteristically more Persian than Chinese. The Sehna knot is always used in Chinese carpets, and there are no discernible regional differences in design and workmanship. While the pile is longer, the knot count per square inch is lower than in most other Oriental carpets. Chinese carpets are easily identified by their basic colors; golden yellow backgrounds symbolize the earth, blue is for the heavens, red the sun, and white the moon.

China is unusual in its cultural solidarity. Unity under a single rule, without divisions, migrations, or infiltrations, has produced an interdependence between the arts and the crafts. It is not unusual for a weaver to use a design from a ceramic bowl, or for an embroiderer to adapt motifs from a garment to a decorative panel because the symbolism is pervasive. To the Western eye, the profusion of decorative elements in Asian art could appear too full and too complicated to grasp in a hurried glance or a quick appraisal. It must be remembered that the pace of the far-distant past was a more leisurely one. Special importance was attached to each object made by the artisan from its inception. Consideration was given to the choice of materials (jade, for instance, would endow the recipient of the gift with noble virtues), to the content of the symbolism, and to the interpretation by the viewer. A gift was more than an expression of sentiment; it could contain a thousand messages. An embroidery entirely covered with separately spaced leaves, peach blossoms, miniature trees, wispy clouds, rippling clouds, a water lily, a lotus flower, an eternal knot, a crooked cross (the forerunner of the Greek key), and the blessed Fu dog

Japanese family crests.

Chrysanthemums. Wood block from a nineteenth-century book. Author's collection.

Studies of chrysanthemums by Pam Arcuri.

would not only be an object of beauty but also would contain symbolic messages to be studied and, as the meaning became apparent, enjoyed bit by bit.

From the jumping-off point in Korea, Chinese influence spread through migration to the Japanese islands. Inadvertently, Japanese art was to play a great part in changing Western sensibilities. Perception and seeing are almost meaningless words without the ability to tune in, to focus, and to recognize new images by their differences. Often the artist totally involved in all subjects related to his art is apt to discover in them elements of design that will contribute to his own creativity. James McNeill Whistler, as an American artist living in England during the latter half of the nineteenth century, is a good example of this point. Dedicated to his art and sensitive to aesthetic values, he avidly collected the Chinese blue porcelain ware available in England as trade items from the Orient. The fragile porcelains arrived wrapped in Japanese prints, which

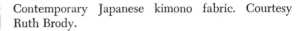

were evidently produced in such profusion that they could be casually used as wrapping paper. What did Whistler and, later, Degas see in these Japanese prints which, when recognized and incorporated in their own work, would liberate other artists, such as Gauguin, Toulouse-Lautrec, and finally Picasso? The radical changes in the positioning of the horizon gave Degas the notion of representing his dancers as seen from above, on a dance floor that appears tilted upward on a two-dimensional surface. And then consider the revelation of Japanese color, flat color without shadows, quiet, subtle color that could whisper softly and still be heard. There is also the Japanese style of patterns imposed on other patterns, dissimilar patterns positioned next to each other, always in a flat arrangement without light and shade. Artists used to the more or less symmetrical compositions of the classical tradition were astonished at the asymmetrical compositions of Japanese prints.

The earliest floral designs from the prehistoric period consist of four-petaled flowers, apricot leaf shapes, vines, and combinations of flowers and phoenixes with scrolled vine patterns derived from China. Later patterns were based on the widely popular honeysuckle motif common in Buddhist art but are thought to have originated in Greece. These honeysuckle designs are very decorative but scarcely recognizable in the manner in which they are represented on the halo-headdresses of Buddhist figures and down the centers of lotus petals, on altars, and in tapestries. They appear flamelike on the halos but are often fluent arabesques on other surfaces, distinguishable as honeysuckle only by their multiple buds arranged like long spokes.

Peonies. Studies from nature.

32

There are many varieties of honeysuckle, and those in Buddhist art are said to be of a type with heart-shaped leaves that grows in profusion in Japanese fields. The motif is also referred to as a palmette and may very well have developed from an entirely different flower. At any rate, the honeysuckle does lend itself to curvilinear vines and adapts easily to left- and right-hand scrolls. Design patterns truly flowered in Japan during the T'ang rule in China, when diplomatic relations were established between the two countries. In A.D. 710 a new Japanese capital city was built in Nara, modeled on a Chinese capital. Many aspects of T'ang culture were transmitted to Japan, and

Japanese brocade. Museum of Fine Arts, Boston.

33

Blackberry blossom (above) and tiger lily. Photographs by Barry Seelig.

master craftsmen from China and Korea, as well as objects from China and from centers as far west as Persia, were imported there. Floral motifs decorated hundreds of objects made for the Emperor: lacquer boxes, hand mirrors, musical instruments, tapestries, and furniture (some of it included tiny cloisonné flower baskets to cover and disguise the nailheads), in addition to gilt-copper and bronze altar pieces, gongs and banners, and even roof tiles. The peony, lotus, honeysuckle, lily, chrysanthemum, wisteria, pomegranate, plum, and grape were used, with the addition of leafy motifs representing the acanthus, hemp palm, bamboo, and Chinese date palm. There were other subjects, too—animals, both naturalistic and mythological, figures and many geometric patterns. Decoration was applied fully in both simple and complicated arrangements: formal symmetry, radial arrangements with a central flower that was expanded indefinitely, revolving arrangements with an open central circular or oval area designed to give the feeling of revolving clockwise or counterclockwise, random scattering of elements and pictorial scenes with a central figure surrounded by a fluid composition of five-petaled flowers and graceful leaves. Less frequently used compositions utilize rows of dissimilar motifs in bands of pattern or grouped in concentric circles. License is taken with many of the individual flowers. Designs are decoratively stylized rather than representative of nature. Many examples known as peonies for want of a better name are more aptly named by the Japanese *hosoge*, meaning a jewel-faced flower.

The peony has great significance in Asia. Revered in China as a native flower and a symbol of wealth and honor, it was often called the "king of flowers" and appeared in many forms. A design might be based upon single or multiple stylized elements; flower heads, buds, seeds, stalks, and leaves might be used separately or in conjunction with one another.

Gradually the Chinese influence diminished, the court moved to Kyoto, and very slowly, during a long transitional period, a Japanese style began to emerge. The most marked change came during and after the unrest of the twelfth-century Kamakura period, when political power shifted from the aristocracy to the military. Expression in art generally reflects its patronage, and design became more naturalistic, changing from the earlier formal symmetry with full stylized forms to a new realism.

Landscape became a frequent theme. A greater variety of pictorial subject matter necessitated different compositional arrangements. The panoramic scene presents problems in representation on a two-dimensional surface. The Japanese artist often emphasized and enlarged upon an intimate detail. Diverse motifs were brought into close focus through discriminate selection. New elements softened the compositions, particularly reeds and grasses; flowers were clustered and field flowers introduced for the first time. Landscape study has a strong emotional effect upon artists. They feel as well as see the strong ebb and flow of rhythmic forces, the nature of color under atmospheric conditions and during the changing of seasons, in addition to finding a creative inspiration in things that grow.

Apart from the shrine hangings and clothing for the aristocracy, cloth woven for apparel was more or less an undecorated twill until the Momoyama period during the sixteenth century. Vast quantities of silk were woven at this time, available to almost everyone for kimonos. These beautiful silken surfaces were decorated with embroidery, hand-painted, tie-dyed, and sometimes impressed with metal foils. Previously brocades were imported from China, but toward the end of the Momoyama period the techniques for producing the most lavish fabrics from the richest materials were mastered by Japanese weavers. Brilliant fabrics were created specially for costumes to be used for women's roles in the No drama. Among the many types of designs were seasonal representations of flowers, grasses, and trees. Similar to the patchwork idea was the use of many different small floral patterns next to each other on one kimono. Sometimes embroidered patterns would be combined with tie-dyed patterns and floral patterns with geometric patterns. Special effects were achieved with stylized flowers, using a method of stitched tie dyeing called tritik in combination with painted dyes and embroidery.

Later, during the Edo period, after the Japanese began to produce cotton, the ikat technique of dyeing was introduced. Ikat is a method of dyeing the threads of both the warp and the weft before weaving to form a design after the piece is woven. Ikat patterns usually include simple, single elements, such as pine trees, bamboo, the peony, or else geometric patterns dyed with indigo blue on white. Ikat depends upon the blurry texture at the edges of the pattern for interest.

Quite different was the hard, precise edge achieved by dyeing through a stencil. To make stencils, several layers of paper were pasted together and strengthened with persimmon juice, which acted as an astringent on the natural fibers of the handmade paper. Stencils of the utmost delicacy were cut, and rice paste, a starch resistant to dye, was applied to the cloth through the cutout areas before the fabric was immersed in the dye bath. Another interesting design technique of this period, one that has been revived by artists today, involved placing pictorial or design motifs within a frame formed of another design pattern.

Flowers were often used in early Japanese family crests. These hereditary crests have the same origins and historical development as other Japanese motifs, but the designs have been reduced to their barest essentials. It was intended that by their strength and clarity one would be able instantly to identify important families, as one recognizes corporate symbols today, without the use of names. The chrysanthemum and paulownia flower (a native Japanese tree having blue-violet flowers in early spring) are insignia representing the imperial household. The most unusual floral aspect of these crests is that they show the reverse side of the flower. The stem and sepal are centered, surrounded by the backs of the petals.

Traditional decorative art in Japan is utilitarian, never frivolous, vulgar, or unnecessary. The design motif is an integral part of the object it enhances. Beautiful objects are considered vital to the daily lives of the people they serve.

Japanese stencil of chrysanthemums. Author's collection.

כל לישון אפס אפי אפי על כמא הראית

אלן. כמכלם ררכויסי, אל ררי וחוושא

The Stylized Flower

Never has the flower been celebrated with more lasting pleasurable effect than in the art of Persia and India, especially during the great periods of Islamic culture, despite the religious prohibition of direct representation. The compound origins of the Islamic culture were derived from the early Semites, the classical Greeks, and the Indo-Persians. Although Arabia gave rise to new religious thought and Arabic was the language through which its ideas were conveyed to other parts of the world, the early nomadic tribesmen contributed little to the cultural flowering that accompanied its rapid spread across sea and land routes; Islamic art owes its richness to many sources. The Islamic world was vast, pushing westward across North Africa into Spain and halfway into France and through Turkey and Persia and India to the East. The outstanding virtue of Islamic culture was its graceful assimilation of the diverse elements in the artistic achievements of the people of these far-distant and varied places. The Arabs learned the art of papermaking from captured Chinese warriors, revived Hellenistic philosophy and scientific knowledge by translating Greek manuscripts, and added much that was new to scientific knowledge, particularly in the field of mathematics. In literature Islam produced *The Arabian Nights' Entertainments* and *The Rubaiyat of Omar Khayyam.* In architecture, the great beauty of the period is best expressed in the mosques; their intricately carved and modeled surfaces display florally inspired motifs and inscriptions in the swirling patterns that have come to be known as arabesques.

The most famous Islamic tribute to the loveliness of flowers is the Taj Mahal at Agra, India. No photograph can do justice to the sense of exaltation one feels in the presence of the Taj Mahal. The entire building of dazzling white marble is inlaid with precious and semiprecious stones of many colors in floral patterns and designs. Set on a raised terrace, high above a river, its domed and minareted façade seems to float in the sky. It was built from 1632 to 1643 by Shāh Jahān as a mausoleum for his wife, Mumtāz Mahal, who, it is said, discovered the means for gathering the fragrant attar from crushed rose petals by placing them in water to allow the essence to float to the top.

The craftsmen of Islam were without peer in their ability to design ornamentation. Prohibited from creating representational art, they relied heavily on abstracting patterns from

Semiprecious stones inlaid in marble in the manner of the floral decorations of the Taj Mahal. Author's collection.

OPPOSITE: Page from a Hebrew manuscript. The foliage scrolls are painted in gold, with leaves and background in magenta. Courtesy *Encyclopedia Judaica.*

German arabesque design, c. 1549.

Exotic flowers. Late fifteenth-century prints.

nature. These mathematicians of the medieval world delighted in the game of assembling tiles in logical systems of mosaics. Of all the arts, calligraphy was most respected because it was considered the invention of God. Granada's Alhambra palace is a superb example of a combined use of geometry, flower and plant forms, and calligraphy in endless variations.

As it could not be rendered naturalistically, the plant became the personal creation of the Moslem artist. He sought to give each flower, each bud, every leaf an abstract, unrealistic appearance. In sculpture or relief, one method of doing this is to render the subject without depth or elaborate detail. Another method, and the one that led Europeans to believe in the existence of exotic flowers, was to make up a plant by borrowing parts from different species and reassembling the sections into an imaginary new one. Often a vine put forth assorted leaves and flowers that might prove astounding to a botanist. A superimposed grillwork might be added over a lacy floral pattern, and when the columns, arches, and ceilings were elaborately carved, the result was a fantasy of decorative effect

Mecca was the religious capital and Baghdad the great

Early nineteenth-century Russian fabric of silk brocaded with metallic thread. The Metropolitan Museum of Art, New York. Rogers Fund, 1948.

Byzantine brocade of the twelfth century. The Metropolitan Museum of Art, New York. Rogers Fund, 1909.

Turkish drawnwork. Author's collection.

marketplace of all Islam. The great caravans and vessels arriving at Baghdad carried silks and porcelains from China, precious stones and rare woods from India, linen from Egypt, gold from Africa, Persian pearls, drugs from Byzantium, and leather from Spain. Brilliant textiles, the celebrated Oriental rugs, glassware, ceramic storage jars, rosewater sprinklers (the rose was the Moslems' favorite scent and was also used for flavoring), gold pendants and bracelets, luster bowls and brass ink containers represented the accumulated wealth of advanced civilizations. It is notable that the Islamic artists did not copy the art created by the cultures they absorbed but carefully selected the most pleasing elements and those that served a useful purpose. The arabesque, for instance, was derived from the Byzantine use of the acanthus leaf, a favorite design form in classical antiquity. Moslem artisans changed the emphasis from the leaf to the stalk, causing the line to undulate or to spiral, depending upon the surface it was to be adapted to, flattening and reversing the form until it became an abstraction from the original. Constant repetition of the form to suit the smallest of objects as well as bands and borders and even entire walls assured the pattern a certain recognizable distinction.

The religious ban on naturalistic representation was not strictly adhered to in decorating objects for secular use. Peoples of different cultures, especially the Persians, the Turks, and the Indians, continued in their own tradition. They were not unbelievers, but luckily they did not adhere strictly to the ban on

Tunisian floral design knitted by Sally Shore.

41

OPPOSITE: "Sintra," an Everglaze fabric print. The design is based on a sixteenth-century tile found in a villa near Lisbon.

Traditional Moroccan jug. Small rosettes are made by pressing a finger covered with slip on the surface of the clay. Author's collection.

Contemporary Portuguese tiles. Collection Helen Kirshner.

Bokharan skullcap embroidered and couched in gold. Collection Mr. and Mrs. M. Kirshner.

Detail of an early eighteenth-century Bokhara embroidery. Author's collection.

idolatry in art work or we would have no record of the preferences and the vigorous activity of the period. How could we know of the Turkish mania for tulips and roses, and the gay parties at which the guests wore tulip colors while strolling in the gardens, if it were not for the court artists? Without this legacy of images, how could we even begin to understand the exquisite leisure of the Persian potentates who introduced Islam to the luxuries of polo, backgammon, chess, and the garden carpet, or imagine the subdued, dreamy Indian gardens influenced alike by Persian example and by the sultry ambiance surrounding a people teetering between sublime mysticism and the ultimate in sensuality? These gardens were generally arranged on a rectangular plan of water channels radiating from central pools with jet fountains and lighted waterfalls. The islands formed by the radiating canals were filled with hyacinths, tulips, daffodils, flowering trees, and bushes. In the center there would be a garden palace with vast airy halls, colonnaded and domed, surrounded by sleeping rooms. The lake palace at Udaipur is a good example, as were, in a later time during the classic period, the Gardens of Shalimar in Kashmir. Paradise was envisioned by the Moslems as a lush, beautiful garden, delicately perfumed by flowers and refreshed by rippling water and rustling leaves, all soothing to the senses. Persian miniatures show carpets used in the gardens as rugs for relaxation, entertaining, playing chess, or courting. The finest carpet ever described was in a record written prior to the Arab invasion of Persia. A fabulous floor covering was woven of silk in the form of a Persian garden. It may very well have been a kilim or tapestry weave because the waterways were couched in silver thread and the gravel paths in gold, the lawns strewn with emeralds sewn to the surface and the flowers composed of pearls and precious stones. The purpose of this carpet was to cover the palace floor in winter so that the Shah might enjoy his spring garden while holding court indoors. More practical examples of the garden carpet were made for less affluent enthusiasts who wished to enjoy the beauty of flowers indoors during the cold and rainy seasons.

Spanish fan. Collection Helen Kirshner.

Important weaving centers flourished in Persia (where contact with the silk trade had been made in China during the Sung dynasty, approximately 960 to 1280 A.D.) and in Egypt, Syria, all of Asia Minor, and Byzantium. Frequent interchange of weavers and artists between these centers makes it difficult to pinpoint proper credit for patterns or establish definite periods for style in the production of fabrics and carpets. On the other hand the ceramic arts flourished during this period and remain today, because they are less fragile, as tangible evidence of great vitality and unprecedented creativity. In the seventh century, before the Arab invasion, Persian design under Sassanian rulers was bold, striking, and imposing in scale. Often fantastic animals were enclosed in roundels, medallions, or other geometric forms in repeats separated by highly stylized floral designs. These textiles achieved a feeling of great authority, a rather splendid arrogance that later, with the advent of more elaborate weaves and the humbler attitudes of the Moslem religion, became subtle and lyrical. The large-scale repeat patterns of the Sassanian period were scaled down in keeping with the prophet Muhammad's command to stress spiritual values. True to Persian tradition, however, the designs remained firm and vigorous. Compartments like the island oases of the formal gardens enclosed unusual winged sphinxes, sometimes geometrically formed around a star, with all spaces between these elements filled with arabesques and foliate designs. Bold angular ribbons delineate the compartments crossing each other to

Pattern of stylized tulips in a seventeenth-century Turkish brocade. Victoria and Albert Museum, London.

Prayer rug with columns terminating in flowers, flower-filled lamp, and floral borders. Osterreichisches Museum für Angewandte Kunst, Vienna.

Ghiordes prayer rug with French-influenced design. Collection Edward Jamgotchian.

form more areas for flower designs. The solid color designs on a contrasting background form silhouettes. Exterior petals and the curving tendrils extending from the arabesques resemble Kufic calligraphic writing. Calligraphy, by definition, means a very beautiful handwriting, decorative, with a great many flourishes. The designer's style is so close to the calligrapher's technique that part of the effect can probably be attributed to the tool used in the performance.

Asian calligraphers use a brush composed of a bamboo holder with many soft hair bristles. For calligraphy, a good brush, no matter what its thickness at the point of attachment, is one that will come to a gradual point when wet. Ink was developed in China as early as 1200 B.C. from lampblack, or from ivory black, which is made by converting ivory into ash by burning. Either material is then mixed with glue of a gum substance and formed into dry cakes. The dried cake is rubbed on a stone, and the rubbings are mixed with water. The black is very rich and is also permanent. A full brush held perpendicularly to the surface of the paper makes a very slender line which gently spreads to the full thickness of the brush as it is pushed down on the paper. The arabesque is an expression of pure rhythmic form easily executed by a designer practiced in the use of a brush.

Another great motif assimilated by the Near and Middle Eastern artists from the Sassanians is the palmette, a stylized form shaped like an open palm or like a hand with the little finger extended. It is known by many names, such as a boteh, a mango, an almond, a teardrop, or a pear. Through the centuries it has taken strange and various shapes, from simple curving lines to the most ornate. Though the palmette may have had its origins in the idea of terrestrial fires, it has been regarded by some as a relic of the ancient Zoroastrian faith of Persia, symbolizing the eternal flame. However, this universally conven-

Detail of floral designs from a Bokhara rug. Collection Mr. and Mrs. William Sadock.

Tabriz rug with floral borders. Collection Michael Silbert.

Bokhara rug design.

Tabriz rug design.

49

Persian garden carpet of the early eighteenth century. Fogg Art Museum, Harvard University. Gift of Mr. Joseph V. McMullan.

Early damask pattern.

tionalized form often mistaken for a leaf has become more or less a leaf outline holding flowers within it. A single flower can form the palmette shape, or it may be composed of multitudes of tiny flowers surrounded by sensuous curves and curls making an entire composition, such as the palmette in the Paisley shawl. The Paisley shawl, named for the Scottish town where it was woven, is noted for its fine thread and subtle dyeing techniques, but the forms are Indian in derivation. Paisley patterned shawls are no longer produced in Scotland. Their tremendous popularity, particularly during the Victorian era, led to mass production on power looms of an imitative product of lesser delicacy and beauty.

More popular than any other symbol, before recorded history and since, has been the ornamental rosette. For everyone, child and artist alike, it is a pervasive stereotype for the word "flower." Any combination of circular or semicircular, short, or intensely elongated elements around a central point is generally called a rosette in architecture, painting, and design. The rose in antiquity was commonly a five-petaled flower, although in the third century B.C. Theophrastus wrote of roses with as many as twelve or twenty petals. The Greek name for the rose was *rhódon*, which the Romans turned into *rosa*.

Oriental symbolism is noted for its frequent use of the lotus flower. Chinese, Egyptians, Persians, Indians, and Assyrians treated the lotus with reverence. It may have made its first appearance as a symbol in Egypt, but the floating blossom is associated with the teachings of Buddha. The lotus appears almost realistically drawn in a large number of Persian carpets, but has undergone an evolutionary design treatment by so many artists, becoming so stylized and conventionalized, that its floral origin escapes the attention of most Westerners.

Probably the rose is the all-time floral favorite around the world. It was cultivated extensively in Eastern gardens and appears over and over again in painting, textiles, and ceramics. Tree roses are frequently seen in Persian rugs. The lily characteristic of some Indian rugs is almost as popular in design. Smaller flowers found in woven fabrics are violets, field daisies, anemones, crocuses, narcissus, and pinks or small carnations.

Silk double cloth in deep blue and cream. Persian, Safavid Dynasty, early seventeenth century. The Textile Museum, Washington, D.C.

Indian painting of the Mogul period. Author's collection.

The Vegetable Lamb. An early European woodcut interpretation of the cotton plant.

Tree of Life. Embroidery detail.

Some older carpets have in their designs the sunflower, an early symbol of the sun and fire, but for the most part the smaller flowers were used for their color associations and beauty. Oriental rugs are often enclosed within many parallel borders containing vines and leaves with flowers and small rosettes. When the vines encircle the field of design without beginning or end they represent the continuity of life.

In 711 a handful of Arabs crossed the Strait of Gibraltar and with the aid of Berber troops from North Africa overthrew the Visigoths on the Spanish peninsula. Spain became one of the main centers of Islamic civilization. The Moslem genius for sifting, transmitting, and synthesizing the cultural forms not only of the Middle East but also of classical antiquity and the Far East had a far-reaching effect on Spain, and Europe was to benefit indirectly. The center at Córdoba, renowned for arts and sciences, was one in which Moslems, Jews, and Christians coexisted, maintaining their individual customs. The last Islamic dynasty, which flourished in Granada for more than two hundred years, produced one of Spain's most artistic monuments, the

Satin brocaded Torah cover from India. Detail.

Palms and cypresses in a late nineteenth-century Indian carpet. Author's collection.

Alhambra Palace. Moslem rule was terminated in Spain when Granada fell to Ferdinand and Isabella in 1492. Moslems who chose to remain and become Christians for a time continued to produce a rich variety of textiles, ceramics, brasswork, and unique luster-painted ware.

Prior to the Islamic conquest Spain was noted for its wool and linen textiles, but it is thought that sericulture and, subsequently, weaving and embroidery with silk were introduced by the Moslems shortly after their arrival. Although the earliest surviving fragments of textiles are from the tenth century, records show that silk factories existed throughout the southern part of Spain at an earlier time. The port of Almería, an outlet for the products of the Moorish Kingdom of Granada, was the most important silk-weaving center. Gold brocade weaving, tapestry, and magnificent embroidery were highly developed during this period. Royalty proceeded under golden canopies protecting them from the Spanish sun, and the processional routes themselves were covered with rich fabrics. European church treasuries as well as royal tombs have preserved a large series of Hispano-Moresque fabrics. One of the robes includes

Embroidered hand-woven cloth hanging. Author's collection.

Detail of hanging shown above.

OPPOSITE: Eighteenth-century Indian elaboration of the Tree of Life theme. Embroidered bedcover or hanging. Museum of Fine Arts, Boston. William E. Nickerson Fund.

the Kufic calligraphy and the geometric patterning of the Moorish tiles surrounding floral designs.

Most of the designs during the Hispano-Moresque period were conceived in the interlaced tile patterns used architecturally, each unit joining another but separated by large straplike bands. Many of the geometric patterns were different versions of eight-pointed stars with curvilinear leaf forms in repeats that gave them a flower form. Generally textiles are the transmitters of style and pattern, but the stucco-plaster carving and tiles of the Alhambra Palace appear to be the source of textile design in Islamic Spain. Large bands of strapwork separated by narrow rows of stepped-up notches, Arabic script, halved and whole palmettes can be seen throughout the Alhambra.

Egyptian designs introduced during this period may have been responsible for the combination of alternating Arabic and foliate stripes, later developing into ogivals with floral patterns. The ogive is a straplike ribbon with pointed arches running between the design units. The continuous ogee, framing a variety of leaf patterns, is also to be seen in the Alhambra designs. The ogee is a sinuously curving, S-like line framing a design element on one side with an opposing S in reverse enclosing it on the other.

The Arabs developed silk weaving in Sicily as well as in Spain. It is difficult to place the source of many designs at this time on the basis of style. Chasubles of the fifteenth century show both Spanish and Italian influences, often mingling fabrics and stitchery techniques from both countries. In many of the vestments the orphreys, or central panels, are heavily embroidered in silk and gold thread with Italianate iconography based on Renaissance painting, whereas the cut velvet side panels with large-scale floral designs are typically Islamic curling acanthus leaves, pomegranates, the endless knot, and exotic flowers. Italy as well as Spain formed an important channel through which Islamic design reached northern Europe.

Damask patterns.

Indian boteh design.

Detail of a Paisley shawl. Collection of
Rosalie Adolf.

Side view of the block used for printing the design below.

Print made from an old Indian wood block.

Realism and Stylization

As the influence of Islam declined in Europe, the flower as it appears in nature gained prominence. Artists of the Renaissance were free to use natural forms and to combine them with the rich elaborations found in fabrics imported from the East. Botticelli's allegory, *Primavera*, portrays a flower-bedecked nymph in a floating gown of filmy tissue embroidered with separated groupings of spring flowers, the most easily recognizable being the garden pink. Paintings by Crivelli and Bellini, as well as others, show a predisposition for rich Oriental cloths of gold and crimson. Vasari describes embroideries for a chasuble and cope executed in Florence from designs by the painter Pollaiuolo. Sumptuous colors used in the paintings of the Renaissance artists corresponded with the fashion for velvets, cut-pile velvets, and silks, most often those of luxuriant Islamic design produced and exported from cities such as Venice and Genoa. The French and German schools of painting also show the preciousness of damasks and foliate fabrics in portraits of kings and saints and special personages of wealth.

Great similarities existed in fashions in clothing between France and England during the Renaissance. Gentlemen in Tudor England in the sixteenth century wore hose and gloves with deep cuffs decorated with gold and silver thread in floral arabesque designs. In a Holbein portrait Henry VIII is shown in a doublet with vertical bands embroidered with interlaced arabesques of gold thread. A portrait painted during the same period by Clouet shows the English monarch's contemporary, Francis I of France, splendidly arrayed in a cloak with immense puffed sleeves inset with black velvet panels embroidered in gold arabesques. When Henry VIII and Francis I met on the Field of Cloth of Gold in 1520, the scene of their encounter took its name from the splendid pageant of fabrics and embroidery surrounding the occasion: on tents, banners, saddle covers, and the decorated costumes of the many noble participants. The robes of Francis I were of gold and silver damask embroidered in colored silks, and his horse's mantle was of blue and gold embroidery with fleurs-de-lis entwined in trelliswork.

Catherine of Aragon, the first wife of Henry VIII, is said to have introduced blackwork into England from Spain, where linens were often embroidered in black thread, possibly in connection with periods of mourning. A young lady's trousseau was composed of fully embroidered bedding, curtains, and

Eighteenth-century French Aubusson chair cover. Collection Melissa Cornfeld.

OPPOSITE: Detail of *St. Agnes* by the Master of the St. Bartholomew Altarpiece. Probably Dutch. Active about 1485 to 1510. The artist gave great attention to the opulent floral damasks of gown and background. Alte Pinakothek, Munich.

Vase and flowers of velvet appliquéd to blue cloth in a seventeenth-century French panel. Victoria and Albert Museum, London.

pillow covers, and linens covering every eventuality. A typical example of Spanish blackwork might be an all-over pattern of arabesques or vines with tendrils and leaves and blackberries, although a great many of these embroideries contained flowers and birds.

During the Elizabethan period the arabesque existed as a linear form enclosing English flowers and other symbols, such as the acorn. Colored threads and metallic thread were still in use. Pattern books were drawn by professional artists. Embroiderers found inspiration in books of flower paintings and in those assembled by naturalists. Whitework, blackwork, appliqué, and canvas needlepoint were all in use at the time.

Persian, Indian, and Chinese influences asserted themselves anew in Europe during the seventeenth and eighteenth centuries, when Asian trade reached its peak in the West. Indian influence was particularly strong in England, where the flowering tree motifs and sprigged and floral fabrics and carpets had great appeal. The Indians under the Mogul emperors encouraged the settling of Persian embroiderers in India, and indirectly transmitted Persian designs to the English market. Similarly, Chinese embroiderers influenced design in Europe by working directly for the export markets of England, France, Portugal, and Spain. Europeans were extremely fond of the characteristic motifs of *chinoiserie*, especially the peony, pomegranate, butterflies, phoenixes, and dragons, heedless of their symbolism. Floral designs were firmly established by the eighteenth century but were further enforced by the popularity of Dutch flower painting and the porcelain flower and bulb containers made in China for the French trade.

Renaissance panel of arabesques and flowers in couched and raised gold and silver embroidery. Collection Jan Silberstein.

Venetians may have formulated the idea for lace by embroidering the surface of drawn work, or by cutting away the fabric around embroidered areas. Whatever its beginnings, Venetian point, or *punto in aria*, literally a point or stitch in the air, is worked with a needle, in buttonhole stitch and with tiny knotted stitches called pips or picots.

Almost all the many variations of needle-made laces can be prepared with a motif drawn on tracing paper. The tracing paper is then placed over black construction paper, and the design is pricked through both sheets. The pricked black paper is fixed to linen fabric. The lace thread is stitched in place or couched to the fabric through the holes in the paper. Open areas may then be filled with netting stitches, bars with picots, or buttonhole stitches appropriate to the design, working across the surface of the paper from outline to outline. When the design is finished, the paper and linen are removed. There are many different styles of lacemaking with as many different names, but more often than not the designs are floral, or floral arrangements in arabesques.

Italy and Flanders both claim to have invented lacemaking. Undoubtedly the lace known as Brussels lace, made by crossing bobbins of thread, is without peer. However, the insatiable desire for effete frills at the court of Louis XIV eventually made France the center of the lace industry. The Sun King nurtured luxury industries, under the impression that the people over whom he reigned had neither feelings nor needs beyond bare subsistence; the arts existed for the glorification and enrichment of the divinely appointed king. Lacemaking suffered great changes after the French revolution. Privilege was abolished

The arms of James I surrounded by exotic blooms and familiar flowers and embroidered on linen canvas with colored silks, wools, and silver-gilt thread in tent, plaited, and long-armed cross-stitches. Victoria and Albert Museum, London.

Early eighteenth-century embroidery of exotic flowers done in wool on a cotton and linen fabric. Victoria and Albert Museum, London.

61

Floral forms reflecting an Asian influence, embroidered on an English coverlet dated 1694. Detail. Victoria and Albert Museum, London.

Silk apron embroidered with colored silks, silver and silver-gilt thread in a variety of stitches, and with laid couched work and raised work. Early eighteenth century. Victoria and Albert Museum, London.

Eighteenth-century fire-screen panel of colored silk embroidery on satin. Victoria and Albert Museum, London.

along with the aristocracy, and the incredible lace luxuries created by specialized artisans were eventually replaced by machine-produced laces.

Tapestry is another art that produces luxuries for the very rich. It is not surprising to find the center of the mille-fleurs tapestries among the great châteaus of the Loire valley in France. It is thought that itinerant weavers wove these huge tapestries (often in sets) right in the châteaus. The most famous, that of the Lady with the Unicorn, is one of a set of six with designs composed of figures and animals set against a rose-pink background strewn with flowers. The Lady with the Unicorn, in the Cluny Museum in Paris, and the Hunt of the Unicorn, in The Cloisters in New York, are precious because they help in understanding the people and their artistic concepts at the close of the Middle Ages. Although the pomegranate (and perhaps a date palm), which appear in one of the tapestries, are of Eastern origin, the plants scattered over the entire background in the mille-fleurs patterning appear to be native to Western Europe. Many of the flowers are easily recognizable. There are clumps of violets, English bluebells, and daisies, primroses, pansies, and

Appliqué work from the Philippine Islands. Early nineteenth century. Muslin on piña cloth. The Metropolitan Museum of Art, New York. Gift of Mrs. Robert W. de Forest, 1923.

Old French fabric with lotus design.

64

narcissus, in addition to familiar trees, such as the oak, holly, elm, and beech. All the flowering plants and trees are naturalistically rendered, unlike those in the stylized fantasies of Islamic art.

A close study of the mille-fleurs tapestries, those of both religious and secular subjects, finds little separation of the background from the foreground. Often the separation occurs as a color change. In the Cluny Museum set, against the rose-pink background (which may originally have been a soft, strong red), a contrasting, small blue-green island floats in the foreground amid a profusion of flowers that continue all around it. The only realization of perspective is the slightly diminished size as the flowering clumps rise to the top of the background. No matter how small the woodland flower, the designer has managed to convey in it a feeling of stateliness. Botanists have identified more than one hundred varieties from the accurate detail and naturalistic coloring. Every petal, every thorn, every leaf with its intricate veining, is a credit to the weavers who interpreted the artist's drawing to perfection.

It appears that not all the tapestries in the set at The Cloisters were designed by the same artist. The first, called the Start of the Hunt, and the seventh, the Unicorn in Captivity, display flowers that are more stylized than naturalistic. They are especially graceful, very slender, slightly elongated, with growth patterns that are semiformal. It is thought that the designer of the first and seventh tapestries might have come from a different locale, and being unfamiliar with certain plants, rendered some from memory or hearsay. This would account for the fact that not all are easily identified. Most of the plants were identified by the staff of the New York Botanical Garden in 1941, who at that time felt that few craftsmen could match the botanical knowledge of the designers of these sixteenth-century

Reproduction of an eighteenth-century French resist print on cotton. Author's collection.

Venetian point lace. Detail of a banquet cloth. Collection Ruth Brody.

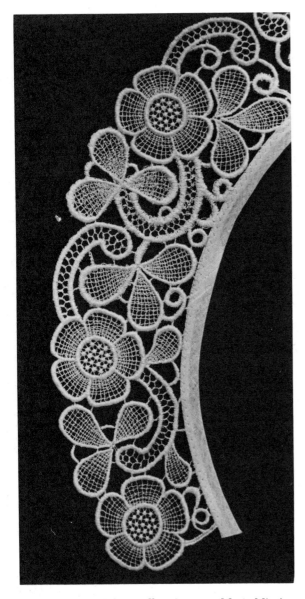

Detail of a Schiffli lace collar. Courtesy Marie Miccio.

OPPOSITE: Floral repeat pattern in lace. Collection Ruth Brody.

mille-fleurs tapestries. Today's craftsmen would have little trouble with the research necessary in rendering flowers in a design. An incredible amount of nursery, botanical, and ecological material is available, but more significant is the loving, intimate acquaintance many people now have with flowering plants.

The work of the mysterious artists of the Unicorn tapestries is all the more remarkable when one considers the highly stylized renderings of the botanical plates in Britain's sixteenth-century Ashmole manuscript. To some, these plants may appear crudely drawn when compared with the naturalistic drawings of the Unicorn tapestries. However, their unsophisticated simplicity could also indicate the possibility of a drawing style not founded on the Greco-Roman tradition of realism. Certainly the early apprenticeship system was quite different from that of the Italian Renaissance. Medieval artists of Northern Europe were not sub-

Eighteenth-century French printed fabric.

Toile de Jouy block print, 1760–1790.

jected to the highly professional training art apprentices were to receive at a later time. A young artist would be employed in mechanical tasks, such as grinding colors and other preparatory chores, rather than in practicing drawing skills that would help him develop his talent.

It was customary to copy existing pictures. Pattern books were kept and used as source material for subordinate detail. An earlier manuscript shows a painter copying from another picture as he works on a panel. The Ashmole manuscript has incidental drawings beneath the botanical studies of floral sprays, household equipment and other implements, in addition to small studies of birds, butterflies, and beasts. These details were included as a handy catalogue of ready reference material for the medieval artist.

It is well to remember that most people reflect environmental influences. Pieter Brueghel, the foremost Flemish painter of the sixteenth century, visited Italy and undoubtedly benefited from the humanistic attitudes of the Renaissance, but was influenced by neither the great Italian artists nor the Antwerp academy. Through minute observation he depicted a living world of peasants at work and play in the fields. On the other hand, Peter

Cornucopias of flowers on a set of eighteenth-century
French tiles. Collection Dr. and Mrs. Martin Greene.

Drawing of violets after the Unicorn tapestries.

Violets drawn from nature.

The Start of the Hunt and (opposite) *The Unicorn in Captivity* from the fifteenth-century mille-fleurs series of tapestries, *The Hunt of the Unicorn*. The Metropolitan Museum of Art, New York. Gift of John D. Rockefeller, Jr., 1937.

Flower still life. Jan Brueghel the Elder (1568–1625). Flemish. © Rijksmuseum, Amsterdam.

OPPOSITE: *Still Life with Flowers*. Jean-Baptiste Monnoyer (1636–1699). French. Alte Pinakothek, Munich.

Still-life oil on copper, signed and dated 1606. Ambrosius Bosschaert the Elder (c. 1573–1645). Dutch. The Cleveland Museum of Art, Cleveland. Gift of Carrie Moss Halle in memory of Salmon Portland Halle.

Paul Rubens did study in Italy for eight years and was an influence on his good friend Jan Brueghel, Pieter's elder son. Jan Brueghel's flower pieces, with their baroque vitality, present so lively an appearance that they seem to move about in their vases with unusual energy.

It is often something of a surprise to discover in these painstakingly accurate bouquets an assemblage of many flowers that bloom at different times of the year. Individual sketches were probably made of each flower at its peak of bloom and a composition arranged at a later time in the artist's studio. The artist was in control of the selection of flowers from his sketches and their arrangement. His own sense of style and feeling for beauty and expression influenced the form each stalk and blossom was to take. When you consider the unknown masters of the mille-fleurs tapestries, the vellum leaves of the Ashmole manuscript, and the Flemish floral painters of the sixteenth and seventeenth centuries, it becomes apparent that all the artists were acutely observant, meticulous to the point of almost scientific accuracy, and yet each expressed himself in a uniquely personal manner. The three examples in different mediums are remarkable. The style of one is neither better nor worse than another, just different.

OPPOSITE: Red wool embroidery in stem, satin stitch, and French knots on a mid-seventeenth-century bed hanging of cotton and linen twill. Victoria and Albert Museum, London.

Cornflower embroidered in tent stitch on canvas and appliquéd to a satin background, c. 1600. Victoria and Albert Museum, London.

Detail of a panel from the Oxburgh hangings (1570) embroidered by Mary, Queen of Scots, and Elizabeth, Countess of Shrewsbury. Tent stitch on linen canvas with embroidery in colored silks and silver-gilt thread. Victoria and Albert Museum, London.

Detail of a late seventeenth–early eighteenth-century English bed curtain. Crewel embroidery on cotton. Museum of Fine Arts, Boston.

The Rose

The wealth in the deep of the rose
Is the wealth within your heart.
Squander it as she does:
In reserve is all your sorrow.

Squander it in a song
Or in a love uncontained.
Do not withhold the rose:
She will sear you with her flame!

GABRIELA MISTRAL
(translated by Kate Flores)

Sweetbrier.

The Rose

If a poll could be taken to determine favorite floral motifs, it is likely that the rose would overwhelm all other flowers in popularity. No other flower has been in the forefront of design so consistently throughout the ages as the rose. Often the form is almost unrecognizable, because since antiquity there have been continual developmental changes in the plant itself. The ancestor of today's luxuriant, multipetaled flower was a small, simple blossom. Difficult though it may be to recognize the rose in some of the oldest existing textile fragments, it is there in a highly stylized form.

Rose. Photograph by Barry Seelig.

Stylized forms are sometimes considered primitive, but in most instances the word is being misused. In some circumstances, particularly among isolated groups, the work may indeed be primitive, the creation of naïve or unschooled artists unaffected by formal tradition. Visual acuity has changed little since the beginning of civilization, and it is quite probable that a stylized version of a flower was a matter of choice, eventually the result of tradition, rather than of naïveté.

However, it appears that even where no textiles have been preserved from ancient cultures such as Babylonia and Assyria, sculpture and written texts indicate that a sophisticated textile industry did exist. Greek and Roman writers speak of Babylonian tapestries, and Assyrian reliefs show patterned clothing that could have been embroidered or the result of complex weaves. It is known that the Babylonians were highly skilled in the needle arts and that their work was resplendent with gold and richly colored thread. Fabrics reclaimed from burial mounds in the Caucasus that date from the fifth century are so advanced in technique as to make one realize how much earlier the developmental processes must have begun.

In the Greco-Roman period ornamental roses were embroidered on the borders of tunics, as well as used decoratively for feasts and festivals. For a very short time the rose's reputation was at a low point among the early Christians because of its association with Roman excesses and pagan festivities. But a

Detail of a Spanish shawl. Collection Jan Silberstein.

Crowned lion and rose in brass. Author's collection.

Fifteenth-century woodcut illustration. A physician is explaining the properties of the rose to a housewife.

secret code of symbols evolved, and the rose, besides being a symbol of the Garden of Heaven and God's grace, was considered to express charity and Christian love. Its petals were believed to represent the wounds of Christ, and the red rose of the blood of Christian martyrs.

Chinese silks designed with decorative roses within squares or medallion forms may have been the inspiration for the European rosette motif. It is also possible that the rose motif and the idea for the rose window may have been supplied by the observations of crusaders returning from the Holy Land. Many medieval churches have large circular windows with a decorative tracery of stone spokes radiating from a small center circle. Chartres, Notre Dame in Paris, and the Cathedral of Rheims are most notable for the beauty of the stained glass and stone tracery of their rose windows. There are fine rose windows in England, particularly at York and Lincoln. In York Minster, there is a Latin inscription reading "as the rose is the flower of flowers, this is the house of all flowers." The state flower of New York is the rose, the state flower of Iowa is the wild rose, and the state flower of North Dakota is the prairie rose. The District of Columbia is represented by the American Beauty rose.

As the national emblem of England, the rose signifies the end of the Wars of the Roses in 1485. The marriage of Henry Tudor

Color diagram from a Berlin woolwork pattern book. Author's collection.

Roses. Berlin woolwork needlepoint, 1850. Victoria and Albert Museum, London.

and Elizabeth, daughter of Edward IV, united the houses of Lancaster and York, with their red and white rose emblems, and changed the fabric of English life. As Henry VII, the new king ordered velvet and cloth-of-gold fabrics to be woven in France with rose motifs. The Tudor rose was adopted as a royal symbol and soon appeared everywhere.

In time most symbolism tends to become corrupted by outside influences. During the reign of Louis XIV, Huguenot weavers took refuge in England and introduced the floral designs of France, particularly the rose, into their designs. The rose design had come to France as a favored motif from Italy with the move of the papal court to Avignon. The weavers had also come from Italy when the silk-weaving industry began in Lyons, and by the eighteenth century French floral designs were a synthesis of many styles. The highly stylized roses of the East gradually developed through the Renaissance into the most realistic renderings ever attained.

Throughout the entire eighteenth century in France the rose dominated textile designs, rivaling painting in the color blending and effects of light and shade that were achieved. The illusion of reality was obtained by dovetailing the colors in slight gradations from light to dark. Philippe de La Salle, a famous designer of the period, was a painter, botanist, and weaver. The naturalism

Embroidered pillow top, 1900. Victoria and Albert Museum, London.

Block print of roses designed in the Art Deco manner by Jeanne Staugaitis.

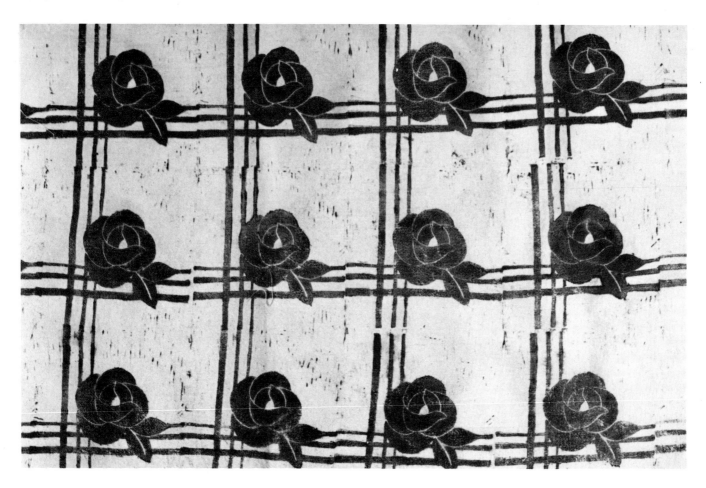

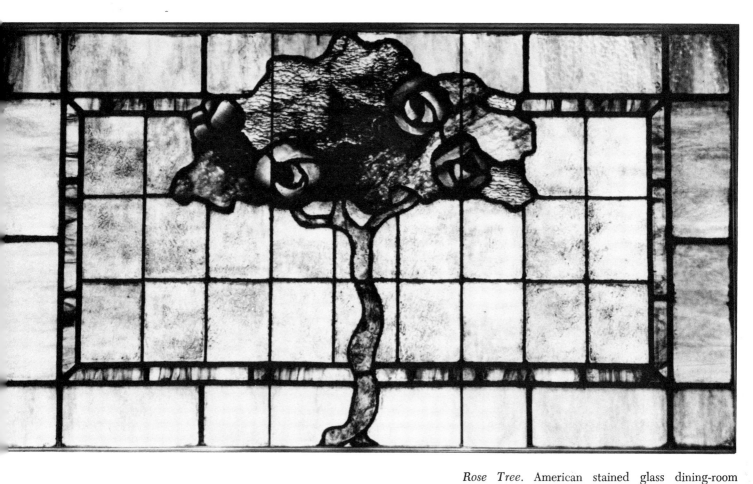

Rose Tree. American stained glass dining-room window in a house built in 1906. Courtesy R. Leigh Glover.

of each flower in his graceful floral festoons of roses was unsurpassed. Another artist of the period, Just Aurèle Meissonier, painter, sculptor, architect, goldsmith, and one of the early creators of rococo decoration, framed floral sprays with scrolls in an asymmetrical formation known as a contrasted balance. Many of the rounded shapes of the scrolls are filled with patterns made by drawn work, lace mesh, or bobbin lace.

With the introduction of the tulip to Europe in the sixteenth century, the rose met its first serious competitor. When the excitement about the advent of the tulip calmed, the rose again gained ascendancy and luxuriated in all areas of design, setting a precedent for popularity during the long reign of Queen Victoria. The industrial age was beginning; the machine was capable of turning out textiles in great quantities, thereby putting them within the means of all.

At the turn of the century the rose continued to hold sway as a poetic symbol of beauty and romance, but all artistic concepts were under fire. Designers were beginning to question the old approaches and search for new ways to express their ideas. The most famous sculptor of the period, Auguste Rodin, in a discussion with Rainer Maria Rilke, said in relation to the teaching of art: "There in the schools, what are they doing year after year . . . they are *composing*. In so doing they learn nothing at all of the nature of things."

Spanish rose medallion of Toledo steel and gilt shows Moorish influence. Author's collection.

Drawing by René Magritte (1898–1967). Collection
Dr. and Mrs. Frederick Mebel.

Roses. Photograph by Barry Seelig.

It must be remembered that Rodin felt that the artist had to
become accustomed to saying everything through the true character of the object, that the essence of reality must be detached
from reality and made into an independent thing, a plastic work
of art. "One should not think of wanting to make something, one
should try only to build up one's own medium of expression and
to say everything. One should work and have patience."

Profoundly impressed by this point of view, Rilke spent a
great deal of his time in Paris visiting gardens and zoos, observ-
ing the flowers and animals, experiences that are reflected in his
poems.

Interior of the Rose

Where for this within,
Is there a without? And upon what wound
Lies a weft so thin?
What heavens are reflected
In the inward seas
of these opening roses
thus reposing? See
How loosely in looseness
they lie, as though never
A tremulous hand could spill them.
They cannot hold themselves still;
Many are filling
Up into their brim and flowing
Over with interior space
Into days, which seem ever
Grown fuller and fuller,
Until all of summer a room
Has become, a room enclosed in a dream.
　　　　　　　—RAINER MARIA RILKE
　　　　　　　(translated by Kate Flores)

Late nineteenth-century Aubusson rug. Collection Edward Jamgotchian.

Rose window from a church in Oyster Bay, New York.

Detail of an American quilt in Rose Tree pattern. Collection Denver Art Museum. Gift of Mrs. Charlotte Jane Whitehill.

Batik design inspired by a rose window.

84

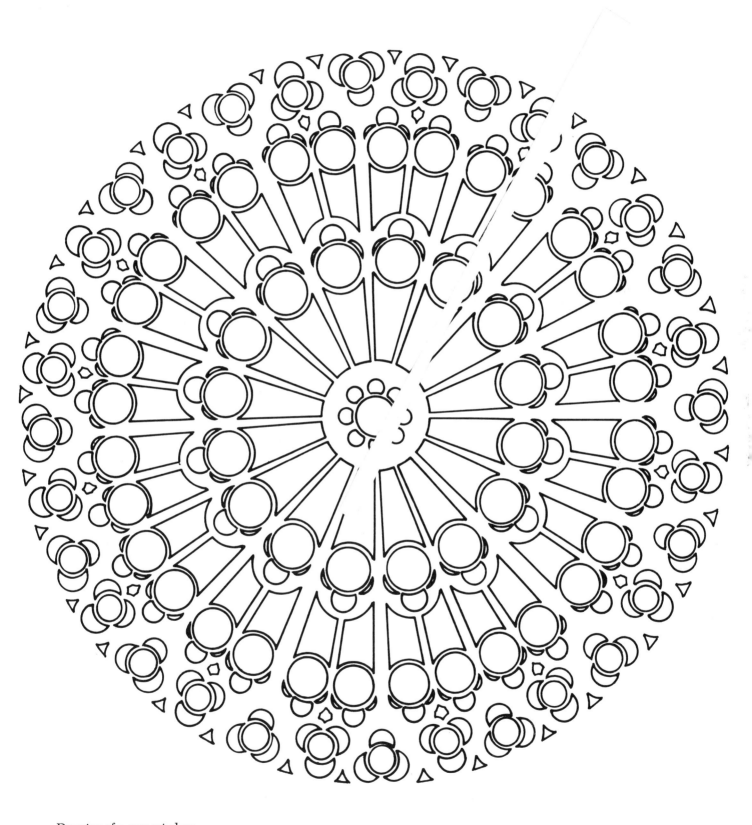

Drawing of a rose window.

The Iris

The flower of French kings is the iris. Its image, like that of the rose, has been used as a symbol and a decoration in many cultures. In France its origin as the symbol of Gaul dates from the fifth century, when the victorious soldiers of Clovis I, who eventually became king of the Franks, were said to have crowned themselves with yellow marsh irises. However, the stylized form of the iris did not adorn the banner of France until the fourteenth century. Early arms of France had a blue field with many small golden fleurs-de-lis, but finally the number was reduced to three. The name fleur-de-lis, often spelled fleur-de-lys, is said to be derived from Loys, the manner in which the first twelve Louis of France signed their names. It was used for centuries on banners and royal scepters with the three large petals symbolizing faith, wisdom, and valor.

There are many kinds of iris. The French fleur-de-lis is thought to be the Florentine iris, native to southern Europe and northern Africa. It has been cultivated mainly for its rhizomes, which provide violet-scented orris powder, a base for violet perfumes. Rhizomes of native American irises, called flags or blue flags, were used by the Indians for medicinal purposes as well as a purgative. Marsh irises also provide a strong black dye. English literature often refers to the fleur-de-lis as a lily. Shakespeare in *A Winter's Tale* spoke of "... lilies of all kinds, the flower-de-luce being one." The Swedish botanist Linnaeus, in his efforts to simplify and systematize plant names, discarded all the old forms and renamed the entire group "iris" after the Greek goddess of the rainbow.

The fleur-de-lis as a heraldic symbol is a conventionalized form. Someone, some place, long ago, in an attempt to create a standard on the battlefield, may have cut directly into fabric following the profile silhouette of a water iris and appliquéd it to a banner, thus establishing its basic outlines. The form has carried on through the years as a highly stylized but conventional emblem used on porcelains, stained-glass windows, engravings, in marquetry, and extensively in embroidery and in printed and woven textiles.

Iris. Photograph by Barry Seelig.

OPPOSITE: Annunciation tracery, 1450. Cathedral of Saint Etienne, Bourges, France. From *Stained Glass in French Cathedrals* by Elisabeth Von Witzelben.

English embroidrey of an iris, 1899. Victoria and Albert Museum, London.

Blue Nun. Painting by Ruth Gray.

Fifteenth-century fleur-de-lis design.

Contemporary knitted fabric with fleur-de-lis design.

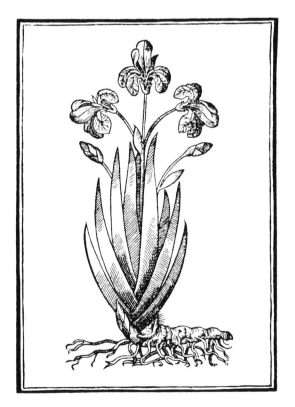

Florentine iris from Mattioli's *Commentaries*, Lyons, 1579.

Interpretations of the iris.

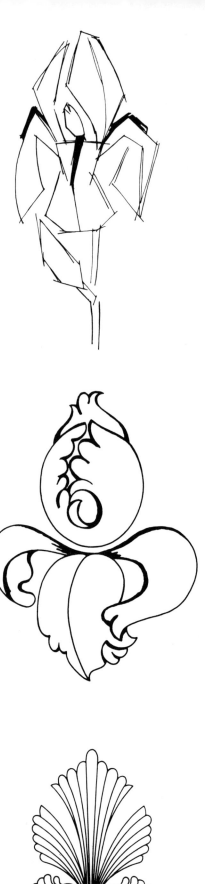

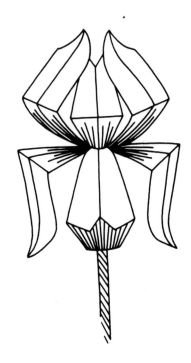

Iris diagrammed for stitchery.

Interpreting the Flower

"He loves me, he loves me not, he loves me, he loves me not." Playing the romantic game of chance with a daisy is a wonderful way to understand the very fiber and construction of a flower. Flowers fall into several categories—those with individual petals, those with petals that are joined together, like gloxinias, or those that are bell-like or funnel-shaped, such as lilies of the valley and morning glories. A single flower head may be carried on an individual stem; so may a great cluster of florets. Hyacinth, phlox, cineraria, and sweet William, among many others, are made up of multiple florets grouped umbrella-fashion on a single stem. And there are flowers like the gladiolus that have, at many points starting part way up the stem, blossoms that bloom and fade in succession. The forms of leaves are equally various: some are notched, divided, ovoid, scalloped, or lobed. Texture also plays a part in the character of leaves and petals. Leaves may be veined, smooth, hairy, shiny, prickly, or bristly.

As an aid to design, keep a sketch notebook of plant forms. Fill it with reference material during the prime of seasonal flowers. Take descriptive notes on color and texture for future reference. The small differences easily observed in nature give a design verisimilitude. In the course of copying from photographs, subtle distinguishing features may be lost in soft photography or through inexperienced tracing.

Press flowers in your sketchbook. Save color swatches and fragments of fabric that are reminders of flowers in all their phases. A tender bud may be quite different from a mature blossom. Make drawings and diagrams. Even a hasty sketch will serve as a reminder or as the basis for future inspiration.

Just as flowers have individual characteristics, so do drawing materials. A medium HB pencil is good for sketching out of doors on a hard-surfaced notebook paper. It is easier to develop detail with a moderately hard pencil because there is less tendency for the work to rub and smear on the paper. Whether working indoors or outdoors, the precise hard line of a pen is excellent for a contour drawing—one made with a single line without using an eraser. Think ahead and observe closely before putting pen to paper. Contour drawing requires practice to enable you to concentrate your eye on the subject matter instead of on the paper. But with coordination and confidence the result is a desired and

Chinese print of a day lily.

OPPOSITE: Swedish counted-thread embroidery. Collection Gunnel Teitel.

93

Day lily. Photograph by Barry Seelig.

much-sought-after personal expression. Preoccupation with drafts-manship is a mistake, producing fussiness, self-absorption, and loss of consideration for the true problem, the problem of content. Too often, especially with flowers, sentimentality is mistaken for content. Anyone may blithely pick up a pen and write a letter, concentrating on the subject matter, giving no thought to penmanship because the symbolic forms are committed to memory and are less important than the content.

People generally consider their own handwriting a unique extension of themselves, to be cherished for its individuality. The same thought should apply to drawing. It has been said that every time we write our names carefully we are practicing drawing. Many cultures consider their drawing no more than a symbolic extension of their handwriting. Egyptian hieroglyphics are a set of drawn symbols written on papyrus or carved in stone and plaster. The Chinese and Japanese use a brush for both writing and drawing. In the Western world the felt-tipped pen can be credited with confusing the graphologists by adding untold vigor and boldness to handwriting and drawing without changing its basic style or character.

If you set aside preconceived notions and limitations, your drawing tool will work with you and for you. Explore its potential by practicing straight, zigzag, and curved lines on newsprint. A line can be broken, overlapped in short strokes, long and sleek, or a series of dots and dashes. It may be nervous, thick and thin, or sketchy. Draw a series of small circles, then some petals. Do not attempt to complete a petal in one stroke. Stop at the tip and turn the paper to a more convenient direction if necessary. In drawing flowers the directional thrust of the stem in relationship to the position of the flower head is the most important line of construction. Most flowers assume very graceful stances reminiscent of the attitudes of ballet dancers, with the possible exception of the swordlike gladiolus.

In order to present an interesting grouping of field flowers, practice exercises in line, following the rhythm and movement of windblown grasses. Select an appealing clump and strengthen some of the lines, emphasizing several that add variety to the rhythmical movement. Using the side of the pencil point, rub it from side to side to indicate the possible arrangements of flower heads.

Almost all flowers are symmetrical, either radially or bilaterally. Radially symmetrical flowers are based on a circle. In perspective the circular form assumes an oval shape when seen above or below eye level. Lightly block out the large areas of the flower by reducing the parts to a series of geometric shapes before starting to consider the intricacies of the contour.

The formal elements of design are line, shape, texture, and color. Not necessarily in that order, but when you think about it for a moment you become aware that almost every two-dimensional expression is composed of these basic properties. Simply closing the two ends of a line encompasses a shape—a form, mass, or area. But one might want a feeling of weightiness in the design, a change of pace from a linear surface.

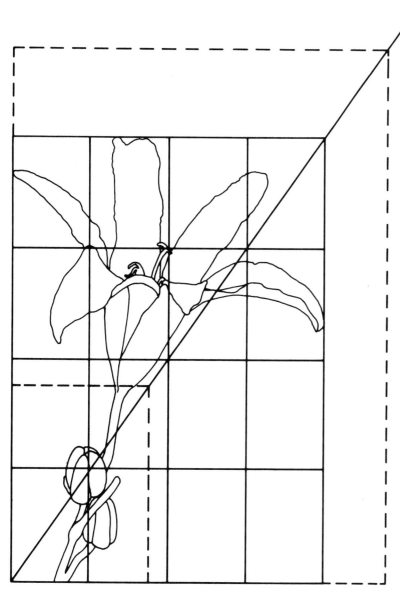

The simplest way to reduce or enlarge a design is to have it photostated in the desired size or, if photostating is unavailable, to use a grid. Place tracing paper over the drawing or photograph to be enlarged. With ruler and pencil draw a rectangle enclosing the design area. Divide it into sixteen equal parts. Draw a diagonal from corner to corner, extending it beyond the enclosed area. A vertical line dropped from any point on the diagonal to a horizontal line extended from the base of the rectangle will produce an area that is larger or smaller, but has the same proportions as the original. Draw a new rectangle with these dimensions and divide it into sixteen parts. Transfer the contents of each section of the original to each section of the new size.

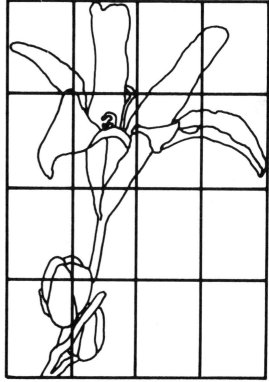

Watercolor is a solid method for delineating a shape without using line. A round sable brush of good quality and correct size will almost automatically make the impression of a petal in a single stroke. Hold the brush saturated with ink, wash, or water-color vertical to the paper. Gently press the tip onto the paper, increase the width of the stroke by slowly pressing down, drawing the brush back at the same time until the stroke presents the desired width. Lift the brush upward sharply to remove it from the paper.

Leaves are made with two strokes of the brush, one on either side of the central vein. Slant the brush away from the stem and pull upward in the direction of the tip. Mass is a term describing the extent of an area. The artist's concern is with the grace and expressiveness of the shape of that area. Although one is primarily involved with the beauty of the positive area, the negative area—the space around the stems, the leaves, and the

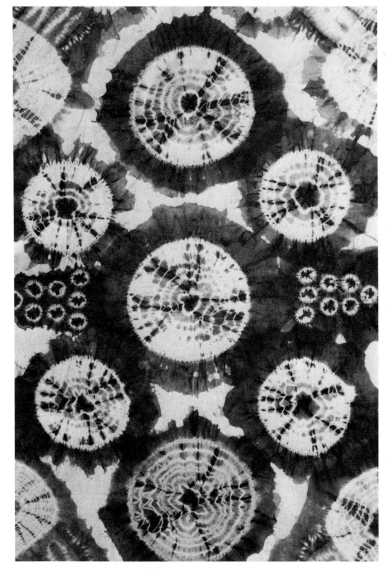

Sunflowers. Tie-dye by Eleanor Bello.

Needleweaving with French knots by Gunnel Teitel.

flower—is just as important. The space between forms creates as much pattern against the background as the forms themselves. Individual petals are important but not as important as the effect of the total silhouette of the flower against its background, whether it is a single flower or a composite grouping.

Cut paper is another approach to defining shape. Matisse, late in life, designed church interiors, chasubles, and windows based on floral forms, working almost completely with scissors and construction paper, finding immense strength and power in the simplicity and boldness of large shapes freely cut. Be careful not to repeat nondescript or stereotyped forms from memory. Heart-shaped philodendron leaves can easily give the appearance of cut green valentine symbols. Select your reference material for its distinctive design potential, or work from nature.

Not every form in nature has design possibilities, although most do. Some are so repetitive as to lack variety. Interest may be supplied through emphasis on detail that invites exaggeration and some distortion. The heart-shaped philodendron can become a bit more idiosyncratic when tension is set up by counter movement. Oppose one gently curving side with an irregular side of some angularity. A geometrically precise daisy is a symbol that can fulfill a function in architectural decoration, in advertising design, or as an element in textile and wallpaper design. Many crafts—knitting for instance—are so formally structured in technique that decoration must be structured to fit the medium. Where the technique is free from technical

Anemones. Positive and negative interpretations in pencil and with brush and ink by Elaine Siegel.

97

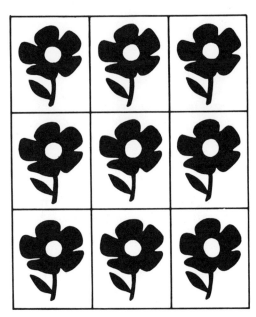

Block pattern.

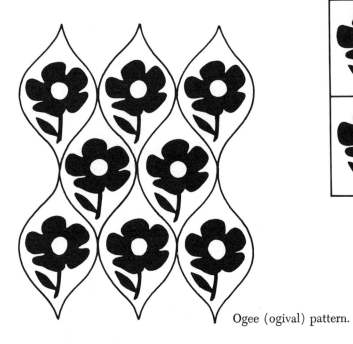

Ogee (ogival) pattern.

Diamond pattern.

Half-drop repeat.

Brick pattern.

Drawing of a seventeenth-century Turkish brocade design in ogival pattern.

An anemone drawn from nature (above) and graphed for stitchery.

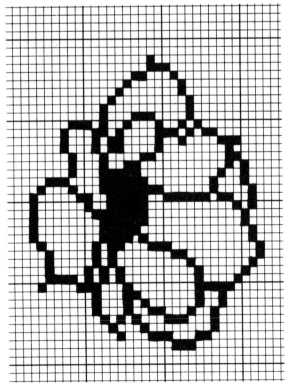

restrictions, as in embroidery and batik, search for the dissimilarities that exist in nature when you create a design.

Floral composition is almost endless in its variety and differs with the purpose and the project. Designing for a wallhanging, a pillow top, a rug, or a bedspread, whether it be executed in stitchery, batik, weaving, or appliqué, is somewhat different from designing for the all-over effect of textile or wallpaper yardage. In the first instance the composition must be complete within itself; in the second, each unit of pattern must be arranged schematically to repeat and join invisibly. Until recently there were recognizable standards for composing within a given boundary. A good composition was like a good story: it had a beginning, a middle, and an ending. The interior construction developed the theme with continuity, flowing rhythmically without running off in superfluous directions that might bring it to a dead end.

The most important principle of design—domination—traditionally entailed a central emphatic theme supported by surrounding material of lesser importance to the composition but necessary to the fulfillment of the meaning. An analysis of floral compositions by old masters shows the centralization of the most opulent of flowers in a massed grouping. Several flowers thrust their heads upward to bring the eye to the outer boundary of the composition and then the eye is returned to the lower portion of the canvas by the device of another object or a single flower placed on the table. Many tiny flowers, buds, and leaves support the central composition, supplying balance and rhythm in addition to a soft silhouette. A bee, a butterfly, or a bug actively conveys the feeling of living vitality.

Composition of this type is formal. Japanese composition is academically informal. Many of the principles of the formal composition are applicable today, but one must reconsider the concept of a beginning and an ending within a given boundary. The rapidity of constantly changing film images has accustomed us to images that hold within them the promise of another. A good design should contain some element of mystery and provocation. Staying within boundaries is restful; deviation can create tension. Always consider the accidental discovery that could be made by breaking rules. A composition that is lively and expressive can hardly be ordered by a set of rules; feeling must come from within.

All-over patterns are made up of units put together in a variety of combinations, but in a certain structural plan in order to form an over-all repeat. The basis of most designs is the block and the brick. The block pattern matches both vertically and horizontally, row upon row, whereas the brick centers the units of one row on the joint of the units in the previous row. The brick pattern turned on its side is known as the half-drop repeat, while the block pattern turned at a forty-five-degree angle is a diamond repeat.

In a sense all structural plans form stripes that are horizontal, vertical, or diagonal, but the most interesting variation is the undulating ogival or ogee framework. The form was often

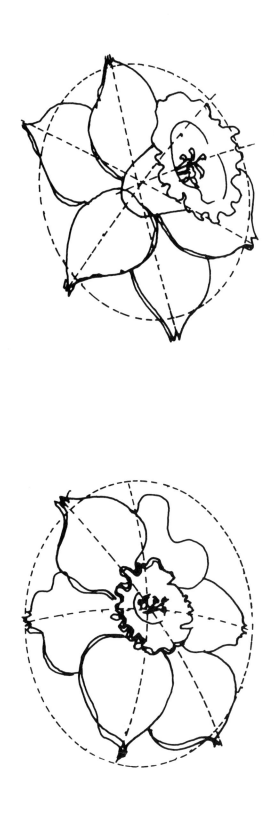

Blocking out views of a daffodil in terms of
geometric shapes.

Laurel motif in a woodblock handkerchief design by Helen Amanda Haselton.

Laurel. Photograph by Barry Seelig.

used on damasks during the Renaissance. The ogee pattern is a curving line consisting of two opposing S curves. Design elements can run with the undulating ogee, with or without a central element. The clever designer can combine plans so that it is very difficult to detect the repeat units.

Scent and color provide a flower with its most provocative qualities. One can know some flowers simply by their fragrance, but to recognize a representational flower one must be able to see its form. The form can stand alone, but color must have the support of the form to give it identity. Many designers feel that color is like icing on a cake. A good frosting can disguise a nondescript cake. If the design is a good one, color will enhance it rather than act as a superficial cover-up. We are always overwhelmed by riotous color in the flower garden. Every color is beautiful in itself, and it is difficult to be discriminating in the face of so moving a spectacle. But color, like the other elements of design, becomes a matter of selection.

Everyone has favorite flowers, but from the point of view of subtle color some of the most distinguished are the anemones. Their color range is very similar to that of azaleas—pink, red, and purple. The great difference in the appearance resides in the color values. Azaleas are very intense. Intensity refers to the brightness of a color. Pure bright colors are saturated with the hue because they are not mixed with neutral or complementary colors. Black, white, and shades of gray are neutral colors. The complement of a color refers to the color directly across from it on the color wheel.

Floral design cut in open line is printed as a single unit at left. The same design, cut as a solid, forms a continuous pattern. Blocks and prints by Barbara Bishop.

Drawing petals with a single stroke of the brush.

Using a cardboard template to make a design.

Mixing a color with its complement softens and modifies its intensity. Green is the complement of red. A touch of green in the red will cause the hue to deepen and its intensity to diminish. The color wheel is a diagrammatic layout of the colors, usually the primary and secondary colors, although many more may be added. Arrange a diagram of the colors in your sketchbook by lightly drawing a triangle. Write down the primary colors first, red across the top point, yellow on the left point, and blue on the right. Secondary colors are made by mixing two primary colors together in equal amounts. Red mixed with blue results in violet; list it on the chart between red and blue. Red mixed with yellow results in orange; list it between red and yellow. Yellow mixed with blue makes green, the third secondary color; list it between yellow and blue.

A tertiary or third set of colors can also be listed. For instance, red and violet mixed in equal parts results in red-violet, a color fashionably called magenta. However, a color wheel has little or no function as a mixing aid. Today, because of the chemistry of commercial paint, it is almost impossible to get a

House plant, a linoleum block print by Martin Ferris, and (below) the design for the block from which the print was made.

pure violet by mixing red and blue. Painters as well as designers do very little basic mixing of color. Water-soluble casein paints, felt-tipped markers, and colored pencils are available in a wide range of colors, as well as a series of warm and cool grays, more than enough for working out designs on paper.

Except for those who are adventurous enough to experiment with dyeing their own yarns and materials, knowing how to mix colors may be less important than understanding how they complement one another when placed together. A written chart is helpful in determining the complimentary and split complementary color schemes. The split complement of a color consists of equal parts of each color on either side of the complement plus the original color from which the complement was determined. A Renoir painting of a poppy field would show a balance between yellow greens and blue greens highlighted with red poppies. A color wheel is a reminder of the wide range of warm and cool colors, of those belonging to the same family and more apt to create a harmonious scheme. Vibrating colors can also be recognized. These are complementary colors of equal intensity and value, setting up a vibration when placed next to each other. But successful designs for needlework and fiber craft are seldom planned in the abstract; inspiration comes from handling the materials themselves. The heaped hanks of yarn in a shop or the samples of threads on a manufacturer's sample card provide a direct way to study color combinations in the reassuring knowledge that the design can be carried out in practice.

A color wheel is also helpful in understanding the results

Chinese blue-and-white jar of the K'ang Hsi period (1662–1722), in prunus pattern.

OPPOSITE: Cherry blossoms handpainted on a page of a nineteenth-century Japanese book. Author's collection.

Prunus pattern embroidered on a mid-nineteenth-century English runner.

of transparency when using dyes for batik or tie dyeing. Generally one dyes from light to dark in washes and overwashes of color. If you start with yellow and overdye with blue, the results will be green. Orange dyed over part of the yellow area will produce a pattern of clear yellow, yellow-orange, and clear orange. If blue, the complement of orange, were to be introduced in equal value over the orange, the color would change to a neutral brown.

Flowers themselves will generally suggest the colors to be used. Try to visualize a flower of a single color, in areas shading from light to dark. A series of about five values is sufficient to produce a feeling of depth and pattern. The monochromatic color scheme of a deep pink rose can be developed by tinting the single color with white. Shade the color with black or with the color's complement. Experiment with black before using it with each color because it has a tendency to change the hue. Yellow will take on a greenish tinge when deepened with black.

Color in design requires quite a bit of experimentation, the very least being the technicalities of the medium itself. Manu-

サクラ

Acanthus leaf.

facturers are happy to supply information about their products on request. Color theories are intended only to be a helpful aid. It may very well seem that a rainbow has limitations, but there will always be another way of looking at it, another light in which it may be seen. The subject of color is by no means exhausted or limited to realism. At different times in the history of pattern, color has been a distinctive mark of the period, usually because the natural materials needed to produce the color were limited to certain areas. Lapis blue, now only a name that identifies a specific hue, originally signified that lapis lazuli was ground up to produce this color. Cobalt was part of the natural clay formula that produced the dark turquoise color of cobalt blue. Turkey's wealth of flowers was recorded on tiles and pottery in turquoise, blue, green, and purple. The Blue Mosque is noted for the color of its foliated Persian tiles. Rich and irresistible color occurs in the fanciful flowers of sixteenth-century tile work, introduced in small quantities of deep red, light blue, and deep blue on a surface of soft, cool grayish white. Some Oriental rugs are noted for a predominance of Turkey red supported by smaller amounts of blue, gold, and white.

Often distinguished color schemes from unfamiliar sources are brought to our attention through the perception of painters. Early in the twentieth century Matisse became acquainted with Persian painting. Through the use of their unusual color combinations, such as pink and red, pink and orange, and pink, magenta, and purple in his own painting, he brought these exotic color combinations to the attention of the fashion-conscious world. Fashion concepts rise and fall, and the search for new forms, new color combinations is ongoing. Innovation and discovery are not the exclusive prerogatives of master painters; individuals experimenting in all the needle and fiber crafts find joyous, satisfying solutions of their own.

Texture is the fiber craftsman's natural ally. Possibly the sympathetic relationship of the craftsman and his medium originated with his love of texture. What could have more texture

William Morris design for wallpaper, "Acanthus," 1875. Victoria and Albert Museum, London.

Part of a bed hanging of crimson satin brocaded in gold, 1805–1815. Ordered by Napoleon I for a room in the Palace of Fontainebleau. The Metropolitan Museum of Art. Rogers Fund, 1944.

than a shaggy rya rug? Not all texture is three dimensional or actively tactile. A craftsman's fascination with texture can be fulfilled on the smooth two-dimensional surface of silk batik, provided the crackling linear detail made by the crushing, sponging, and texturing of the waxed surface do not overwhelm the content of the design. Flowering plants are well provided with texture. Embroiderers will easily find texture in the intricate veining of leaves and petals. The short, flat stitches aptly called seeding describe pollen-bearing anthers in a flat texture. French knots at the center of a daisy have a raised dimensional texture. There are obvious textures and delicate ones, smooth textures and rough textures. Even the invisible stitches a quilter uses to define a white-on-white pattern produce a subtle texture. Appreciate the gift of abundance, but use it with restraint.

Photograph of a rose.

Photograph with grid.

Outline drawing.

Diagram of color values.

Making stitchery designs from a photograph. An outline drawing can be made by laying tracing paper over the photograph. To establish a range of color values graded from light to dark for needlepoint or embroidery, tape the tracing paper to the top of the photograph and mark off the divisions of a grid along one side and the bottom. A ¼″ grid will give detail; a ½″ grid allows a broader interpretation. A T-square will assure parallel lines. In the absence of a T-square, mark the grid on all four sides and draw connecting lines with a ruler. Five or six values will produce a well-rounded form. Pencil shades of gray can be used, but lines drawn both closely spaced or far apart, crosshatching, and variations on the diagonal are easier to interpret. Prepare a key to the values in advance. The grid can be used for shades of a single color or for several colors.

110

Stitchery diagram.

The Plates

2

3

4

5

6

7

8

9

10

12

13

14

15

17

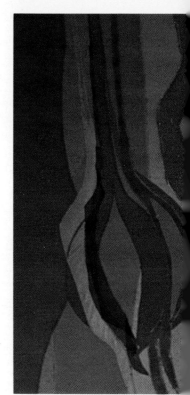

18

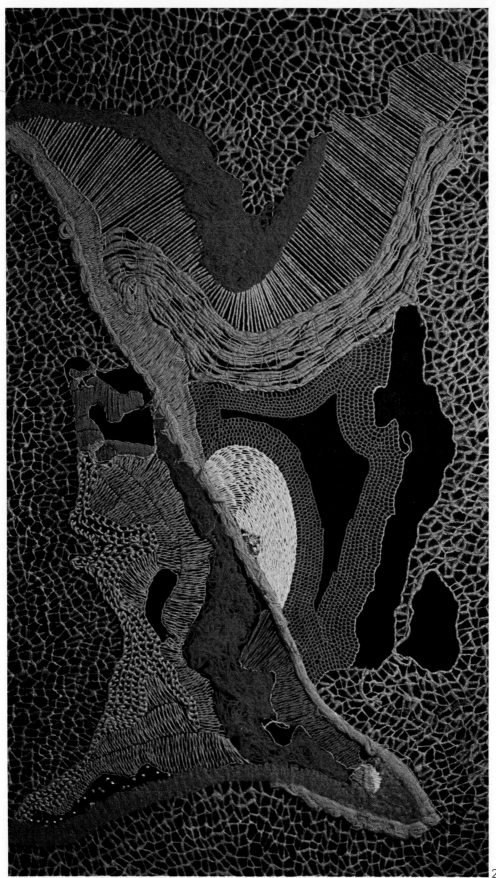

20

21

22

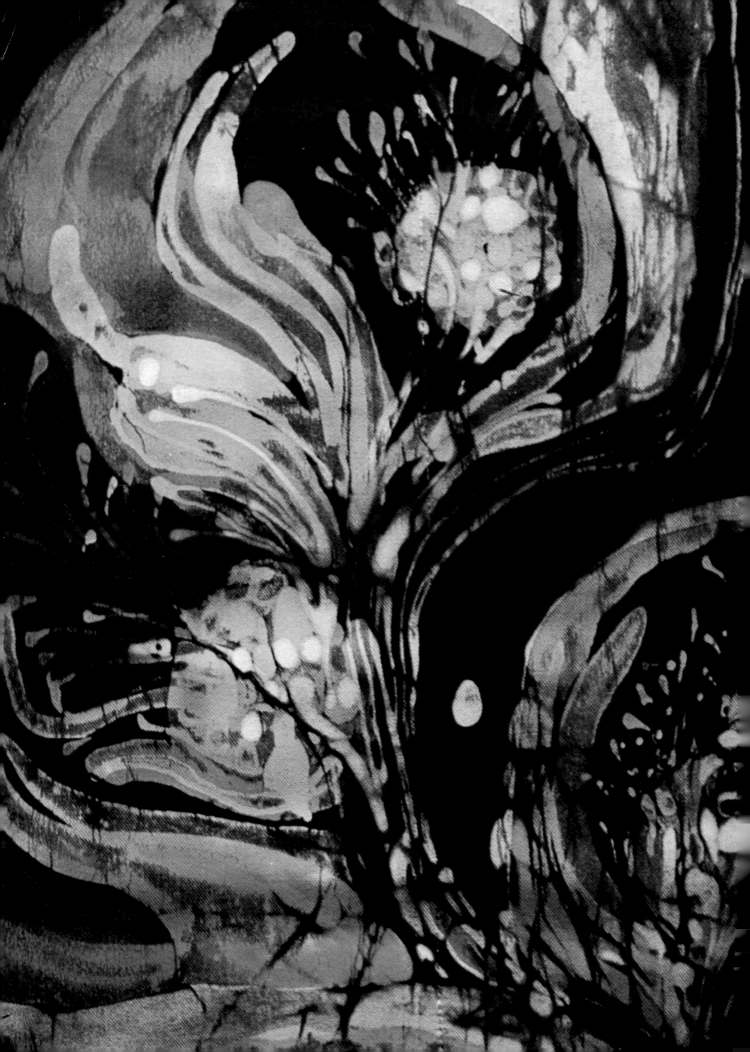

Floral Design in Dyed and Printed Fabrics

The origin of using dyes to decorate fabric is rather obscure, but the process probably preceded both spinning and weaving. The earliest idea for patterned design may have occurred when someone noticed the image of a fallen leaf or blossom recorded on tapa cloth left out to dry and bleach in the sun, thus marking the beginning of a very direct form of floral decoration. In any event, many dyeing techniques offer unique opportunities for freedom and spontaneity in design. Tapa cloth (which is made by pulping tree bark in water), animal skins, and felted hair were often colored and patterned by primitive peoples. Although the technique survived the longest in Oceania, implements for making bark cloth have been discovered around the world. Berry juices were often used for coloring. Eventually designs were carved on printing blocks, or painted directly on the blocks and then offset onto the fabric. Other effects were created by embossing leaves in a resinous material to form a mold for printing, by various forms of tie dyeing, or by using resist methods such as in batik.

Tie dyeing and resist dyeing are practiced with flair by the Yoruba women of Nigeria. Stylized flowers, trees, and birds are sometimes used in areas divided into squares and rectangles like patchwork. Flower designs are simplified four- or eight-petaled sunflower forms with small or extremely large center circles. These single-colored designs are highly textured. Both the background and the flowers have interior designs composed of dots, close parallel and diagonal lines, small open circles, and the grid impression of a screen. The designs of indigo-dyed Adire cloth (in which patterns are achieved by resist methods) are formal and conservative, with the single color contributing a sophisticated mark of identity.

Butterfly design on an Indonesian tjap, a copper hand tool introduced about 1850 to speed the batik process by stamping the wax resist on the cloth preparatory to dyeing. Author's collection.

Floral symbols from the Admiralty Islands.

Involved patterns made with an inordinate degree of skillfulness and showing exceptional detail are to be found in Indonesian batik. This wax resist process has a long history which started in India or China, but examples are also to be found as far away as the burial sites of Peru. Indonesian batiks were introduced into western Europe after the Dutch colonization of Java and Bali. If at first Europeans found it difficult to accept the unaccustomed designs, their appetites for the exotic and their delight in the richness of the crackled veining of batik eventually produced a demand.

Indonesian patterns are nonfigurative in accordance with Moslem law. The craftsmen reduced all natural forms to symbols and then arranged the symbols in patterns that repeated continuously. The effect sometimes appears to be that of an all-over texture rather than obvious motifs. Some of the patterns are drawn as seen from above and formed within circles and squares. Blossoms and seed heads are redesigned so that the stamen of the blossom is exaggerated in length and often made long enough to form a star or a cross. These units are again regrouped into a rosette formation; sometimes the groupings also take the shape of a cross or a star. These in turn are contained within a square or other geometrical shape. Typical also of Indonesian patterns are diagonal stripes of sufficient width to contain small geometric floral repeats. Backgrounds often contain multitudes of small floral designs within a palmette.

Early batiks were worked on a cream-colored cotton fabric, and the decoration was restricted to the shades of blue obtained from indigo. In some examples a reddish brown is also used, thus adding black where the brown overlaps the blue. Much later yellow was added to the color scheme. A length of batik fabric was worn wrapped around the body, somewhat in the manner of a sarong or sari. Gold embroidery was used on fabric intended to be worn for ceremonial purposes. Interestingly, there is a distinct change in color value and pattern direction on each half of the fabric because the garment is meant to be worn in different ways at different times of the day.

Contemporary batik and traditional Javanese batik work are so different as to be considered two different crafts, even though resists and the same scribing tools are used. The use of thin silk makes it possible to apply the resist on one side only, and today a brush is often used for this purpose instead of the copper tjanting cup.

Textile painting and resist dyeing permit the ultimate in freedom for the fiber craftsman. The method is direct and spontaneous, offering an opportunity to make changes and design decisions while the work is in progress. A fully colored sketch may be used instead and copied in the traditional manner. In copying, without the vitality of an unhampered line, there is a tendency for the effect to be static. Initial sketches and sample color experiments are excellent aids in planning designs, but there are unexpected surprises in working directly in batik that add to the excitement of the medium. One can take advantage of the unexpected and absorb the accidental by incorporating it into the design.

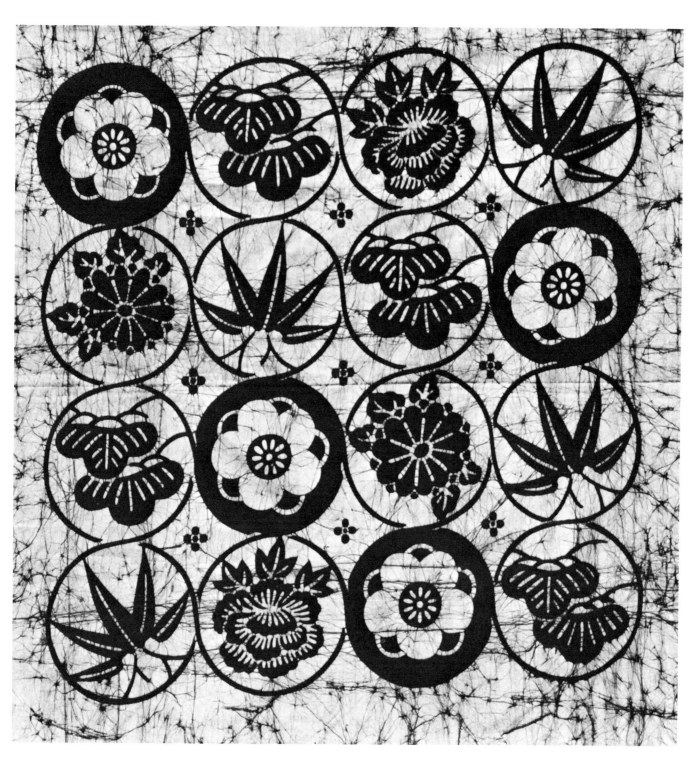

Batik fabric. Collection Mr. and Mrs. M. Kirshner.

Indonesian batik fabric. Collection Mr. and Mrs. M. Kirshner.

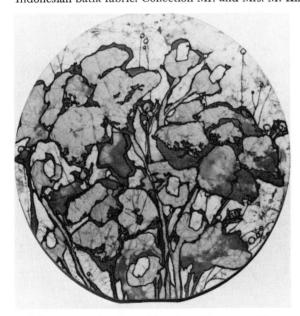

Celebration in the Round by Sara Eyestone. Photograph by Joan Kingdon.

Quite different and more varied and delicate are the floral effects made possible by printing with wood blocks on woven cotton cloth. As late as the thirteenth century Marco Polo spoke of cotton as vegetable wool growing on trees; even today "cotton wool" is a not uncommon expression used to describe unspun cotton. It is said that King Solomon used cotton hangings in his temple in 950 B.C. Supposedly the cloth came from Phoenicia and Egypt, but as both countries had trade relations with India at this time it is possible that the fabrics for the temple were Indian. The use of cotton was mentioned in Indian records as early as 3000 B.C. Probably the first peoples to cultivate cotton were those living along the banks of the Ganges River.

Fabrics known as calico, chintz, gingham, madras, and muslin (frequently printed with floral patterns) originated in India, where a tradition of nearly five thousand years of weaving cotton on handlooms is unparalleled. Think of a spool of cotton thread, spun to needle-eye thinness, and imagine the incredulity of European weavers in the time of Marco Polo when they

Bouquet with Ceramic Vase by Viggo Holm Madsen.
Batik on cotton by the direct-paint method.

were introduced to gauzelike muslins woven with a continuous thread miles long. A traveler returning from Dacca described these muslins as the work of fairies rather than men. It seems almost beyond belief that a hand-woven, hand-spun fabric more than 60 yards long and one yard wide could be made from one pound of cotton. Imagine a warp and weft count that began around 100 and sometimes ran as high as 300 threads per inch. People speak of the filmy linens of Egypt, the flower-silks of China, and the woven wind of India. Surely, with such poetic descriptions of these fabrics, a natural choice for the designs to appear upon them would be those inspired by the flower, whose sole purpose seems to be to please.

What batik is to Indonesia, block printing is to India. India may very well be the original home of the printed textile. Originally the designer's effort was to distill the essence of the flower without direct representation. With time, the designs have become traditional, with each designer basing his work on that of previous designers. Some of the traditional blocks contain narrow border designs, others have individual groupings of flowers in the shape of an oval or a diamond on a single stem. Another type is a design unit with a central undulating vine having stylized flowers of many kinds on either side. These units when joined often form an interior border. A little palmette is another favorite Indian motif. There must be thousands of ways designers through the centuries have devised floral arrangements to fill the interior of a palmette. Sometimes they have a serrated edge and a border within a border with bands of small foliated designs.

Designs will vary considerably from area to area, but because the method of block cutting is about the same, the technique has a certain uniformity of style. After the design is drawn on paper it is then pasted on a hardwood block of suitable size. The design is cut into the wood with a gouge, to a depth of about a quarter of an inch. Iron strips are sometimes set into the block to form some of the pattern. Most blocks have their backs shaped so that it is possible to grasp them with one hand. The black, reds, and blues of natural dyes are the most usual colors, although today aniline dyes have replaced natural ones. Printing with natural dyes requires that the cloth be prepared in advance with a mordant to make it receptive to the color. To print the designs, the cloth is laid on a table, over a padded surface of several thicknesses. A stamping pad saturated with dye is used for applying the color to the block, which is then pressed on the cloth. The block is often hit with a wooden mallet to make a more solid impression. Not more than one or two colors are used together; those most commonly used are red and black.

During the Middle Ages European textile printers employed interesting, if somewhat tricky, practices in their desire to imitate expensive fabrics from the Far East. Gold and silver dust was scattered over thickened dyes before they were completely dry. The luxurious effect of velvet pile was obtained by spreading finely powdered wool over the pigment, sometimes thickened with oil or varnish, while it was still wet. In Germany a special set of instructions gave details for copying the flowers and

Geraniums. Batik by Marie Miccio. The resist was applied with a handmade tjap (opposite).

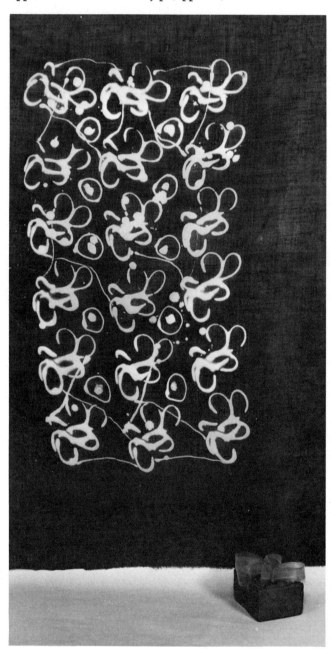

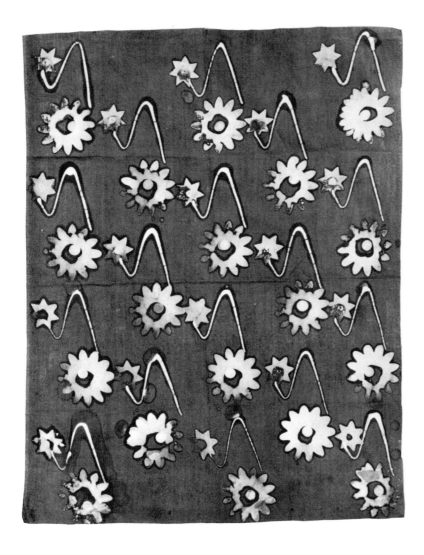

Left and below: Floral batiks created with found objects by Sal Minore.

Tjap used to create *Geraniums* batik. The plasticine block holds the plastic strips in place and provides a convenient handle.

Gladioli. Block print (right) by Irene Shtohryn and (below) the design for the block.

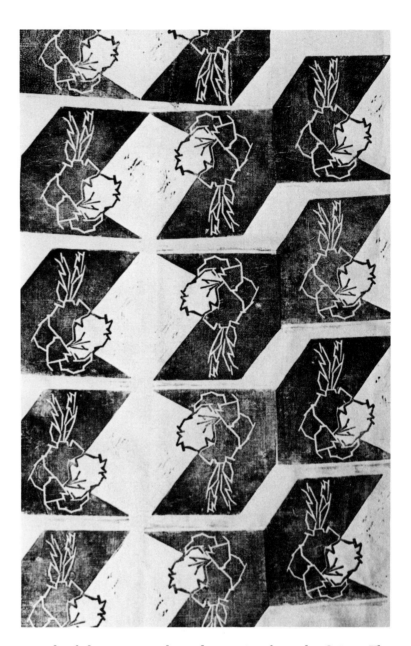

animals of the expensive brocades coming from the Orient. The printing blocks of this period more or less imitated the designs in these woven fabrics.

One aspect of block printing during the fourteenth century was to prove a revolutionary aid to embroiderers. As the craft began to take hold among people of increasing leisure, outline patterns were printed on cloth to supply the demands of home embroiderers. Elaborate embroidery hitherto had been an enrichment for ecclesiastical robes and the ceremonial vestments of royalty. The religious tenets that influenced a great deal of medieval European design were retained in the restrained classical attitudes of the Renaissance. Rising secularism, however, was responsible for a livelier vision, and design gradually became less geometric, less formal, more natural. Flowers conveyed romantic love without artifice.

Floral batik on silk by Libby McGregor. Courtesy
Helen Kirshner.

Folk Art Forms and Themes

In the Americas the fiber arts were most advanced in pre-Columbian Peru, but flowers were rarely used in the designs until after the Spanish conquest. Peruvian design generally included geometrically stylized animals, birds, and figures representing gods and demons. Silk was imported to the Americas from China and the Philippines. Reflecting this Asian influence, design elements began to include chrysanthemums and phoenixes, probably in imitation of imported Chinese embroideries.

Flowers were also unusual in the crafts of the North American Indians until the eighteenth and nineteenth centuries, when the Iroquois began to decorate clothing with glass beads brought from Italy as trade items. Mohawk and Tuscarora moccasins were designed with heavy floral motifs of crudely threaded beads raised from the surface by padding. Floral designs were also embroidered with moose hair, which took dyes easily. These embroideries show a strong French influence, because Indian girls and women were taught by nuns in the newly established French convents. Later the Tuscarora achieved very realistic floral effects with more refined techniques and the use of colored beads in many graded shades, apparently in imitation of European art forms.

The Navajo and the Zuñi are silversmiths. Although they both make squash blossom necklaces, there is a distinct difference in their approach to the craft. The Zuñi cut and shape stones into intricate mosaic patterns, using the silver to hold and contain the pieces. The Navajo, using heavier silver, shape hollow beads and blossoms and place more emphasis on the sculptural quality of the forms.

Early settlers brought most of their possessions with them from Europe. Later the demands of the American market were met by imported goods from France and England. Even when calicoes were first printed in the colonies, the processes and

Sunflower design carved on an oak panel from a seventeenth-century chest. The Metropolitan Museum of Art. Gift of Mrs. Russell Sage, 1909.

OPPOSITE: Seat cover in eighteenth-century American crewelwork. Wool on linen. The Metropolitan Museum of Art. Gift of Mrs. J. Insley Blair, 1946.

Peruvian Indian water-storage container. Ceramic, with decorative motifs of Spanish Colonial influence. Author's collection.

American salt glaze jug with blue flower design. Author's collection.

designs were imported from Europe. It was not until the advanced technology of the twentieth century that American design developed in a unique direction, especially after the development of screen printing. Today the designs and techniques of the ages—photography, needlework, embroidery, weaving, batik, collage, assemblage, painting, patchwork, and block printing—may be combined or adapted and photographically transferred to screens for mass printing on fabric.

The most exciting work done in America's formative years was in the folk art tradition. The bed was probably the single most important piece of furniture in an Early American home, and quilts and coverlets were functional and beautiful, designed with warmth and affection by the women of the household. Their work was free and meaningful, commemorating American history and family events with yarn and scraps of cloth. Geometric patchwork patterns were worked out with the utmost frugality, and cheerful appliquéd flower gardens brightened otherwise sparse interiors. The patterns of some flowered quilts identify the area where they were made. The tulip motif was a favorite of the Pennsylvania German region. The rose, however, was everyone's favorite, including each and every type, from the cactus rose to the tiniest rosebuds. Geometric patchwork arrangements of petaled flowers derived from the profiles of tulips and lilies.

Woven coverlets, particularly those woven on hand looms with Jacquard attachments, for the most part had floral designs in two or three colors. These coverlet designs frequently repeated floral carpet patterns. A great many were on double-woven cloth, so that the coverlets were reversible. The Jacquard

Post-conquest Peruvian tapestry. The Metropolitan
Museum of Art. Rogers Fund, 1908.

Thistle and teasel. Plate from the Ashmole portfolio.
© Bodleian Library, Oxford.

OPPOSITE: Guatemalan teasel brush used for raising
the nap on woven blankets. Author's collection.

Thistle. Photograph by Barry Seelig.

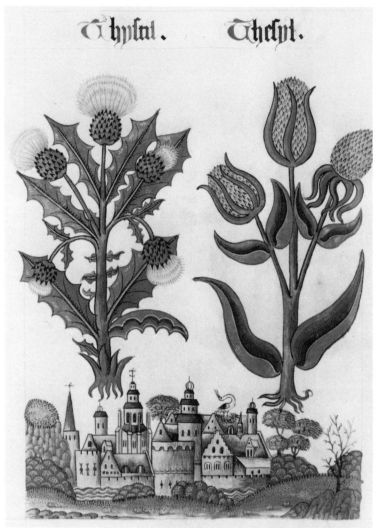

attachment was made up of a series of overhead punched cards
that controlled the warp threads in the desired pattern. Most
coverlets were signed and dated by the weaver, in addition to
carrying the name or initials of the individual for whom the
coverlet was woven. Colors were predominantly blue and white,
sometimes with the addition of red. Later other colors were
added.

During colonial days most of the dyeing and spinning took
place at home. Generally the white or natural-colored warp and
weft threads in these coverlets were spun of cotton. Contrasting
weft threads were wool, dyed with indigo and cochineal red.
The sophisticated central floral designs of most coverlets were
of European origin, hardly in the folk art tradition. The borders
were quite personal. For instance, the Gilmour brothers of
Indiana regularly wove a border pattern of colonial houses
separated by picket fences with a design of trees behind them.
Other weavers were fond of the American eagle, oak leaf and
acorn borders, and floral borders with the rose predominating
as a theme. Both itinerant weavers and weaving families became
obsolete at about the time of the Civil War as the country
turned to mass production.

Very few homeowners could afford the luxury of wallpaper,

Silver belt buckle and clasp of mother-of-pearl inlaid in silver. Zuñi. Collection William Sadock.

but they were eager for the cheerfulness of color and the liveliness of decoration. The itinerant painter was a welcome visitor in rural areas. He brought with him patterns for quilts, designs for hooked rugs, and stencils for decorating the walls, the space above the fireplace, and sometimes the floors as well. Basic patterns were floral wreaths, baskets of flowers, urns with floral bouquets, oak leaves, occasionally pineapples and willow trees. The stiffness of these generally symmetrical designs was offset by the charm of their simplicity and ingenuousness. There is a relationship between the stencil designs and appliquéd quilt patterns, although the borders and narrow vertical strips of design between pattern lengths in the wall decorations would indicate a desire to imitate wallpaper.

These same itinerant painters often excelled at portrait painting and freehand decoration of household items. However stiff and somber the portraits may appear, furniture decoration was intended to enliven simple interiors and beautify chests, chairs, and tables made at home or purchased from the local carpenter. Pennsylvania Germans were noted for their dowry chests and wardrobes, which were hand-painted. Each chest was lettered with the name of the marriageable daughter for whom it was made. Many of the traveling artisans' designs had their origins in European folk art, but these country craftsmen adapted freely from memory and added other purely decorative elements to round out the compositions. Although many pieces were stenciled, particularly in New England, others were painted freehand. (Chairs stenciled in the manner of Lambert Hitchcock, who opened his Connecticut factory in 1825, are still being mass-produced.) Flowers were a favorite subject among the designs of both stencilers and freehand painters.

One of the finest artistic accomplishments of home handwork has been called yarn painting. Needlework is a medium of expression that has the delicacy necessary for making floral portraits. Since the Renaissance, when embroidery became a secular art, the flower has been for the most part one of its dominant themes. In some forms, such as samplers, flowers play a decorative role subordinate to a central text that is often more flowery than the flowers themselves. A sampler is, after all, a sketchbook, a record of favorite motifs and patterns. The word "sampler" is derived from the Latin *exemplar* meaning an example or a model—the designer's test sample. At first, as ideas occurred or were suggested to the embroiderer, they were recorded and stitched with no particular plan. The embroiderer then used these samples as reference material for designing other pieces. Sometimes early samplers were symmetrical in arrangement but nevertheless contained a great variety of forms, providing ample subject matter for the designer. Later samplers became more formalized and then conventionalized, usually with a central theme surrounded by a decorative border, but still made use of many traditional—and some experimental—stitches.

Eventually samplers were used as a method for teaching stitchery to young girls. Samplers were often sewn at school

Navajo squash blossom necklace. Collection Theda Sadock.

Adaptation of the onion pattern to a cotton fabric.
Courtesy Ruth Brody.

Meissen porcelain in traditional onion pattern. Author's collection.

Hooked rug. American, nineteenth century. Courtesy Doris Leslie Blau.

Washington pattern coverlet in dark blue and white, double woven by hand on a Jacquard loom. American, 1837. The Toledo Museum of Art. Gift of Edward Drummond Libbey.

Appliquéd and quilted bedcover in tulip pattern. Collection Dr. and Mrs. Martin Greene. Detail.

Stained-glass tulip window from a house in Brooklyn. Collection Mr. and Mrs. William Sadock.

as a stitchery exercise and as a lesson in the alphabet as well. For the most part, American samplers were influenced by English and German needlework, until the beginning of the nineteenth century, when landscapes were introduced. Hills and dales were placed across the bottom of the samplers, with trees and flowers springing up along the edges. Borders changed too. Instead of the Tudor rose of English samplers, the flowers pictured were those common to the American garden. Later examples became increasingly realistic, making use of free curvilinear forms.

The Spanish influence evident in Mexican and Central American embroidery makes use of brilliant colors and floral motifs more flamboyant than those found in examples from northern countries. In Mexican embroideries the stylized flowers appear to be modeled on the hibiscus, pressed flat or as seen from above. Characteristic of Mexican embroidery are long, flat satin stitches, often in silk or in silky mercerized cotton thread. Primary colors combined in large flowers closely massed with little background space between them give a full, rich effect of gaiety and strength.

Tulip design in a Pennsylvania German appliquéd
quilt. Collection Dr. and Mrs. Martin Greene.

Persian palm lily pattern appliquéd on linen in an early-American quilt. Victoria and Albert Museum, London.

Needlepoint chair seat. Boston, eighteenth century. Museum of Fine Arts, Boston. Gift of Mrs. Kemmand Winsor.

Pansy. Photograph by Barry Seelig.

Detail of a crewelwork bed curtain. Massachusetts,
eighteenth century. Museum of Fine Arts, Boston.
Gift of Mrs. Daniel Staniford.

Detail of a crewelwork petticoat border in wool on
linen, said to have been made by Tabitha Lincoln.
Museum of Fine Arts, Boston. Gift of Frank Lus-
combe Tinkham.

Bedcover stenciled in red, green, and yellow-orange.
American, c. 1830. Metropolitan Museum of Art.
Rogers Fund, 1944.

Basket of Flowers. Traditional American design
based on English exotic flower forms.

Hand-painted dower chest, c. 1780, Lancaster
County, Pennsylvania. The Metropolitan Museum of
Art. Gift of Mrs. Robert W. de Forest, 1933.

The Fabric of Contemporary Design

The printing process combined with the commercial practicality of cotton substantially influenced design during the Industrial Revolution. The introduction of appealing floral cotton calicoes and chintz fabrics from India threw the textile manufacturers of the mercantile countries of Northern Europe into a flurry of activity. So great was the demand for these gay prints strewn with floral sprigs and provocative exotic flowers that late-seventeenth-century weavers of silks and woolens in England as well as in France protested the competition.

London was for many centuries an important textile center, specializing in linen cloth, worsteds, and woven woolens. With the exodus of the Huguenots from France, still another textile center, one noted for silk weaving, was established at Spitalfields in England. Spitalfields designers concentrated on dress silks that followed the trends of high fashion in France. They developed an unprecedented delicacy of design using naturalistic flowers in fresh colors brocaded on a light, thin, lustrous ground. An act of Parliament in 1700 forbidding imports of block-printed fabrics from India had the effect of intensifying efforts to improve production of printed textiles in England through the study of Indian dyeing and designing techniques.

Schools of design were established in England, Scotland, and Ireland by 1740, encouraging artists to work for the textile industry. Manufacturers were interested in suitable designs for carpets, wallpapers, table linens, and fabrics for an ever-increasing market. Until the development of aniline dyes about the time of World War I, the Indian methods of mordanting for color receptivity and the resist techniques prevailed. Color was derived from the madder plant to make black, brown, red, and purple, indigo supplied blue, and weld (a form of mignonette) yielded yellow. A great many other plants were experimented with and used; sometimes the colors proved impermanent. The dried bodies of cochineal insects, which thrive on cacti in North American desert areas, were used to provide a strong red color.

Copperplate printing was an improvement over printing with carved wood blocks. Introduced in the middle of the eighteenth century, the process was similar to the intaglio method of printing etchings. The copperplates were as large as thirty-six

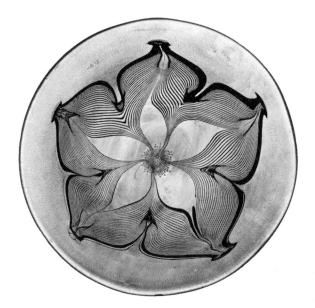

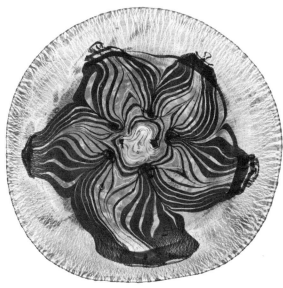

Louis Comfort Tiffany favrile glass plaques. The Metropolitan Museum of Art. Gift of H. O. Havemeyer, 1896.

OPPOSITE: "Queen's Pattern." Brocaded silk designed and woven by pupils of the Spitalfields School of Design for the Great Exhibition of 1851. Victoria and Albert Museum, London.

Designs by William Morris. "Compton," an 1896 wallpaper design (right) and "Honeysuckle" chintz, 1876 (opposite). Victoria and Albert Museum, London.

William Morris stained-glass window, 1872–1874. Victoria and Albert Museum, London.

inches, lessening the need for frequent changes in the position of the fabric as it was being printed. More delicate detail was also possible. A floral bouquet drawn in all its detail in pen and ink, complete with fine veining and slender spiny thorns, could be faithfully reproduced by a copperplate etching.

Never was the flower in design more popular. Flowers were easily adapted to the curvilinear forms of the baroque style and the excesses of the rococo. Large and small, budding and full-blown, flower forms presented a lively appearance of movement and three-dimensional roundness. Flowers were naturalistically represented in color and form. Bouquets were gathered together with representations of satiny ribbons floating and undulating as though suspended over an electric fan; Cupid's bow and quiver were an addition to the designs, a mythological reminder of the romantic symbolism of flowers; cornucopias overflowed with flowers; trellis and pillar alike were garlanded, twined, trailed, and festooned with flowers. Roses mingled with jasmine, hops with ribbons, day lilies with freesias, leafy ornaments with arabesques. There were infinite combinations of geraniums and lilacs, thistles and lilies, carnations and lace, passion flowers and sunflowers, baskets and vases of flowers, feathers and flowers, peacocks and flowers, pagodas and flowers, poppies and moss

roses, pansies and roses, ferns and ivy, wildflowers and grasses, flowers and grapes. The ubiquitous floral wreath encircled everything: eagles, presidents, bright sayings and homely mottoes, horses, and tombstones. It appeared on trophies, linens, plates, portraits. Never before had there been so voracious an appetite for the prettiness of fabrics patterned with floral and foliate designs. Objects, from the smallest soap dish to the lowliest spittoon, were also decorated with flowers. Eventually society, by its demands on an uncontrolled technology involved in mass production for the greatest profit, created not only human misery in suffocating factories and intolerable slums but a shoddy, vulgar product as well.

The eminent Victorian designer William Morris foresaw an appalling future of wasted human potential, despoiled ecology, and economic injustice in the rapidly growing industrial environment. A return to medieval principles of morality and craftsmanship seemed to him a solution to the problem. He felt that life itself could be a work of art if one was surrounded by the useful and the beautiful in everything from the smallest object to the largest. He considered the position of the artist and the craftsman most enviable during the Middle Ages, a period when the designer was his own man and not a tool of the machine. Part of his idea for maintaining the dignity of the artist was for the designer to carry out his own designs, whatever the medium.

In keeping with his consuming passion for medievalism he had built for himself and his wife a house conceived in a style characteristic of architecture during the thirteenth century. The garden was planned along the lines of a medieval garden and

English ironstone ginger jar in Mandarin pattern.

Flowers. Andy Warhol, 1967. Acrylic and silk-screen enamel. Courtesy Leo Castelli Gallery. Photograph by Eric Pollitzer.

OPPOSITE: *Mixed Flowers in a Vase.* Pierre Auguste Renoir (1841–1919). Museum of Fine Arts, Boston. Bequest of John T. Spaulding.

Playing cards with designs based on the poppy, tulip, dandelion, and cyclamen.

Goblet designed in tulip form by Karl Köpping, Berlin, about 1895–1896. Kunstindustrimuseet, Copenhagen.

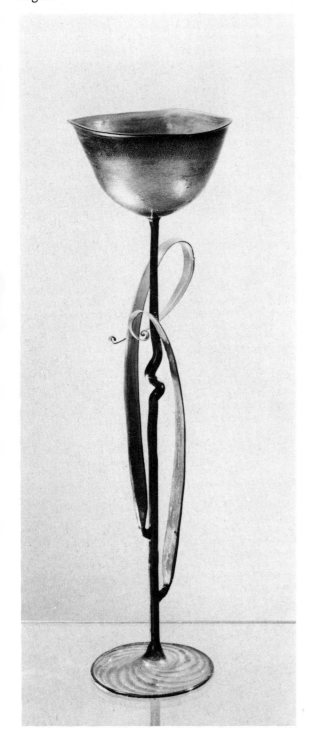

was divided into smaller squared gardens with long grassy walks. Rose-covered trellises enclosed beds of day lilies, nasturtiums, hollyhocks, and sunflowers. Creepers of honeysuckle grew outside the door, and wildflowers filled the corners of the garden. All these flowers were a source of inspiration for his wallpaper designs, woven and printed fabrics, and carpets.

Morris, John Ruskin, and other intellectuals of the mid-nineteenth century were confronted with the unique situation of an unprecedented mass market with tastes conditioned by the cheap products available. Manufacturers had abandoned individual design and craftsmanship in favor of reducing costs by copying patterns, slicing and chopping at existing plates to fit new fabric widths, and resorting to quick and crude block-cutting and plate-making. Among artists, the floral realism that had reached a feverish pitch by mid-century was characterized as vulgar, demoralizing, even counterfeit. More and more William Morris came to romanticize an ideal of medieval craftsmanship. His early designs were spontaneous and naturalistic but later adhered to strict structuring of the repeat patterns. No sudden breeze would ever give them the effect of wafting

Art Nouveau baby cup. Collection Helen Kirshner.

Book page decoration in Art Nouveau style.

undulation. The flowers are stylized and combine many varieties. In some the central portion takes the form of the palmette filled with leaves and berries. In a lecture in 1879 Morris explained that patterns are meant to fill the eye and satisfy the mind but must maintain a certain mystery. The pattern should not be so obvious as to be understood at a glance and just as rapidly dismissed.

The aestheticism of Japanese screen painting beginning to filter through the consciousness of Western artists at this time, revealed the possibility of a new order in flower painting, but its simplicity never affected Morris's work. His designs are rich and full, creating a completely textured surface.

While William Morris tried to re-establish a working tradition modeled on the past, other artists began to create a different style of design. The machine was of the present, and to turn one's back on it was, after all, a failure to recognize its possibilities. The irony of Morris's dedication to hand craftsmanship was that economically it could never be within the reach of ordinary working people. Designers of the Art Nouveau period at the turn of the century determined to work with the advancing technology by beautifying architecture and bibelot alike to create a unified order. Architects, designers, painters, and craftsmen tried to establish a related harmony within all the arts. Table settings were designed to harmonize not only with the draperies but with the hostess's gown and her accompanying jewelry as well. Every item within an interior reflected the over-all design. Ornament is defined as a part or an addition that contributes to the beauty or elegance of an object. If any word could possibly describe the sinuous, attenuated forms of Art Nouveau, it would be elegance, for the word is so subjective and at the same time suggestive of great style.

The organic structures of Art Nouveau designs were founded in the crowded patterns of William Morris but were more closely allied to the work of those of his associates who had achieved softer floral forms, almost linear in pattern, on simpler backgrounds, influenced in part by the Japanese prints of Hokusai. Japanese artists reflected an intimate, personal experience with nature without copying its surface appearance. One art stimulates another, and many botanists, in the desire to supply motifs for the artists, researched natural subjects, wrote scientific articles on horticulture, and prepared illustrations of natural forms that had never been seen before. The most unusual ones had the greatest appeal for the Art Nouveau artist. He delighted in the languorous shapes of exotic hothouse plants and reveled

Flower pistils and pollen grains in silver and pearls in a hairpin designed by Helen Kirshner.

Tiffany lamp of favrile glass and bronze with a lily-pad design base.

in pale hues. Certain flowers keep recurring in these designs—
the lily, the orchid and, less often, the sunflower because of its
less adaptable radial form. The tendril of the vine becomes
much more interesting than the leaves, and the bud of the
flower more suggestive than the fully formed blossom.

English wallpapers and fabrics were famed and imitated
throughout the world. Arthur Mackmurdo was a pivotal figure in
the transition from the influence of Morris to the fluidities of
Art Nouveau, affecting many aspects of contemporary design.
His fabrics evoked a sensation of rapid movement, with flowers
and birds appearing to fly in formation. Foliage darted about
like flames, and at times the whole design was set in perpetual
undulation across the surface. His work to some extent antici-
pated that of Charles Francis Voysey, who created a different
surface of equal importance in which the shapes of overlapping
enormous flowers tend to mix and create a neutral, over-all,
two-dimensional ground. Morris had designed from the point of
view of subject matter placed on a background. Voysey con-
structed an entirely new surface with the curvilinear forms of
the flower.

Problems of form and function, form and its relationship
to materials were under discussion at this time in Europe. It is
more than likely that the inventions of the Art Nouveau designers later acted as a catalyst upon the thinking of the Bauhaus
intellectuals. Belgium's Victor Horta designed buildings in which
the architectural detail literally grew out of the ground in a
delirium of developing tendrils. For the Art Nouveau designer
the search was for the new idea, the novel idea, not deliberate
sensationalism, but a definitive turning away from the direct
imitation of nature on canvas and in machine-made furnishings.
New construction materials had caused frenzied reorientation
among designers. Malleable iron easily fulfilled the premise that
form should be adapted to material.

After viewing examples of the new forms, the Belgian
designer Henry van de Velde observed, "It was as if spring had
come all of a sudden." And indeed it had; even the sophisticated
Parisians must have been astonished at the sight of Hector
Guimard's rather antediluvian blossom of painted cast iron and
colored glass, its extended arms sprouting at the entrance to the
subway system. The fledgling electric light bulb, shamefully
naked, assumed many disguises. Most common was the flower.
Swaying stalks carried the wiring, and glass blossoms concealed
the bulb. An occasional petal was turned back on itself to
release more light.

New-York-born Louis Comfort Tiffany probably made the
most important American contribution to Art Nouveau. Like
William Morris, he began his career as a painter. After extensive
travel that included the study of the stained glass of medieval
cathedrals, Tiffany returned to the United States in order to
concentrate on experiments in glassmaking. He too was concerned with designing for the increasingly popular electric light.
Typical of his work is his wisteria lamp of the favrile glass and
bronze that is synonymous with the Tiffany name. From the
top of its domelike shade, a pattern of deep blue wisteria blos-

Blue-jean embroidery. Courtesy Vera Maas.

Contemporary African printed fabric. Collection Mr. and Mrs. M. Kirshner.

soms and green leaves falls from a network of pierced branches. The lamp standard resembles a tree trunk right down to its circular base of tangled roots.

Favrile, a term coined from the Latin *faber*, or craftsman, was adopted as the trademark for Tiffany's transparent or opaque glass in which the colors flow into one another to produce iridescent and textural effects. Tiffany's love of flowers and gardens led him to attempt the merging of the indoor and outdoor world through the design of large windows. Transparent and shimmering, the windows responded alternately to daylight and, after dark, interior lighting. The changing sources of light produced different images. His famous Oyster Bay window is almost a companion piece of the wisteria lamps. Great clumps of wisteria hang from a trellis that forms the leading of the window. In the middle distance is a view of Oyster Bay, Long Island.

Tiffany experimented with a great variety of possibilities: different layers of color, draped molten glass, and the inclusion of chunks of chipped glass, pebbles, abalone shells, and even semiprecious stones. His casement magnolia window has three slightly concave panels with an over-all arrangement of white magnolia blossoms done in a folded drapery technique which adds texture. Others of his windows feature snowballs, tulips, poppies, and symbols of autumn and winter. Flowers were transformed into a highly personal vision of open-form vases with bulb-like bases and ruffled rims. He designed not only glass but whole interiors and their contents—rugs, candlesticks, vases, tapestries, chapels, and his own home at Laurelton Hall, down to the smallest household items. He designed a series of buttons that he called "little missionaries"; the tiniest one was intended to convey the story of the importance of creative living.

Just before and after the outbreak of World War I, influences from different parts of the world produced a climate of excitement, an intellectual ferment. Charles Rennie Mackintosh, a Scottish architect and designer of furnishings and decoration, caused a reaction to the fantasies of Art Nouveau throughout Europe with his design for the Glasgow School of Art. He pioneered in the treatment of the function and geometry of architectural space. His designs for fabric as well as furniture were concerned with rectilinear and other geometric forms. Germany and Austria supported various arts and crafts movements sympathetic to the rationality of Mackintosh's designs. Associations of architects, craftsmen, and manufacturers were formed to solve the problems of producing designs that were both functional and aesthetically pleasing. By 1920 students and teachers of the Bauhaus in Weimar, Germany, had successfully developed a connection between industrial technology and aesthetic taste that abandoned completely the florid fantasies of the nineteenth century.

Cubism was initiated by Picasso and Braque in 1908. German painters were combining intense color with Cubist geometry. Two outstanding flower painters of the period were France's Odilon Redon, who used color with powerful intensity, and the German expressionist Emil Nolde, a flamboyant colorist

Basket of Tulips. Hooked rug by Helen Jacoff.

with great verve and freedom of style. Italian Futurism was concerned with the persistence of movement and the multiple images of objects in motion.

The Russian Ballet was to exert a tremendous influence on all the arts, in part due to the vibrant personality of its director, Sergei Diaghilev. In 1909 Diaghilev presented the first European performance of the Ballet Russe in Paris. Until this point set designing had consisted mainly of imitation fern and trellises, and the costuming had been elaborate and frilly, but Diaghilev had an instinct for impressive theatrics and employed the leading artists of the day to design costumes and settings. They reacted against what was then termed "bourgeois realism," changing not only decor and choreography throughout the world but women's fashions and interior decoration as well. The new set designs were expressive and bold, heavily outlined in black, created in a wholly new scale of colors. Flowers, though stripped of their tendrils and elaborate complications, were still a favorite motif, however. Formalized geometric shapes, often evocative of the rosette or flattened daisy, symbolized the idea. African art was also being introduced to Europeans, who found their broad stylized forms a challenge.

In 1922 the opening of King Tutankhamen's tomb in Egypt revealed new sources for designers. The favorite flower here was the lotus, boldly symbolized, usually in profile. Seen from above or in profile, the flower easily lends itself to stylization. Discoveries of pre-Columbian cities in Mexico and South America re-

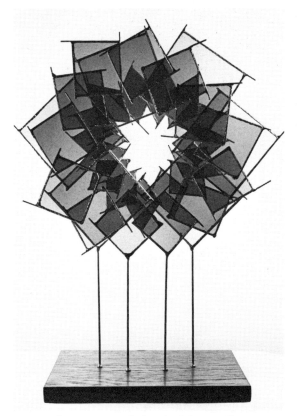

Organic form in stained glass by Mariette Bevington.

165

Spring Bouquet. Printed fabrics freely cut and machine stitched to a dotted background. Martha Miller.

Rya rug. Design inspired by floral forms in a drapery fabric. Gunnel Teitel.

newed interest in themes from these civilizations. Brilliantly colored two-dimensional flowers and the ziggurat shapes of the Mexican pyramids influenced package designs and dress fabrics. Frank Lloyd Wright fostered interest in American Indian art and culture by using the geometric Aztec motifs as architectural detail.

Black and silver were hallmarks of the Art Deco period, which was initiated by the international exhibition in Paris in 1925. Silver gilt and black enamel, chrome and plexiglass, bakelite and platinum were new materials put to use by Art Deco designers, who borrowed freely from elements of design from all over the world. By the 1930s there was a definite commitment to streamlining and a passionate affection for forms symbolic of speed. Smooth shiny surfaces with clearly incised parallel lines and concentric circles thrust upward and radiated outward. When representational motifs were used, they consisted of bold flowers and leaves, fruit, sometimes gazelles, even wolfhounds. Concurrent with the Art Deco period was the Bauhaus influence and its dedication to a purity of line uncluttered by decoration.

Until the end of the nineteenth century, when the painter became concerned with his medium and himself and began to convey his inward impressions, all design forms had been rather rigidly conventional. But Claude Monet's water lilies are more of an atmospheric impression painted in a highly personal manner than a direct representation of flowers. The Egyptian lotus,

Tulip Crest by Jan Silberstein. Trapunto and braided chain stitches on muslin.

although stylized, is a pictorial representation, used again and again until the style has become a convention. Many painters were more sympathetic to other modes of expression. Emil Nolde, through strength of color and the vigor of his brushstrokes, sought to describe the vividness of the flower rather than its botanical detail. Paul Cézanne gave his pictures more substance and depth by using warm and cool colors in advancing and receding planes without shadows. He advised artists to see in nature the cone, the cylinder, and the sphere, paving the way for Cubism and the abstraction of forms from subject matter. Picasso and Braque arranged new surface treatments by combining other mediums with paint. Collage materials and the assemblage of objects introduced the idea of the juxtaposition of unusual subjects and dimensional forms.

Georgia O'Keeffe is a daring flower painter. Perhaps influenced by photography, she seems to make, from something very small, a cropped enlargement stripped of extraneous detail. Her color often reflects the brilliant white light of her New Mexican environment.

If, after all, it appears that the flower in design has followed the course of social and art history (and it is apparent that the flower is the subject matter of about two-thirds of all design patterns and motifs), then in a sense it has been an important measure of the aesthetic sensibility of the world. Throughout the centuries flowers have been a favorite subject of still-life

Winter Flower #2 by Michael Cornfeld. Flat-woven wall hanging with pickup loops and warp wrapping.

167

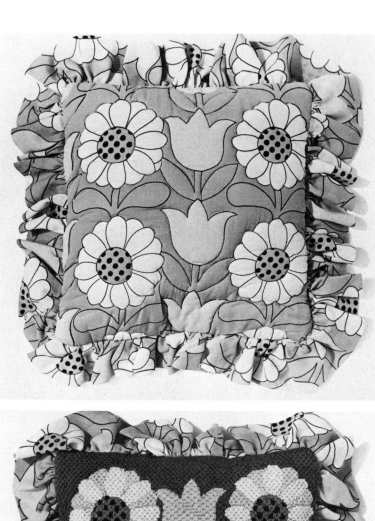

Two sides of a pillow. The bargello stitchery design on one side was adapted from the printed fabric on the reverse. Gunnel Teitel.

Tie. Fabric design by Marimekko of Finland. Courtesy Design Research.

OPPOSITE: *Peony* by Anna Abraham Gardner. Fine marker and Dr. Martin's dyes on waxed rice paper. Detail. Photograph by D. Preston.

Art Nouveau design by Carol Whitman.

ABOVE AND OPPOSITE: Art Deco designs.

painters, and recently of photographers. The flower is unquestionably the single design element most prevalent in fabrics and wallpapers.

Many artists and craftsmen have felt an uneasy ambivalence about the flower as subject matter because sentimentality so often seems to permeate thought about its obvious beauty. In addition, overwhelmed by the patterns and designs of mass production and the photographic images of television and movies, most subject matter without the power to shock tends to lose the power to attract attention. Nevertheless, the flower is still a positive challenge for painters and printmakers, still the undisputed favorite for designers of dress fabrics, accessories, wallpapers, and household linens. Appliqué, stitchery, and needlepoint designers created more new floral patterns for the market during the past decade than in all the previous ones. It is safe to say that the flower is still a powerful presence in the world of design. The multitude of forms in which it has been presented continues to offer a wealth of inspiration, a challenge to the designer to find new ways to use and interpret its provocative forms.

171

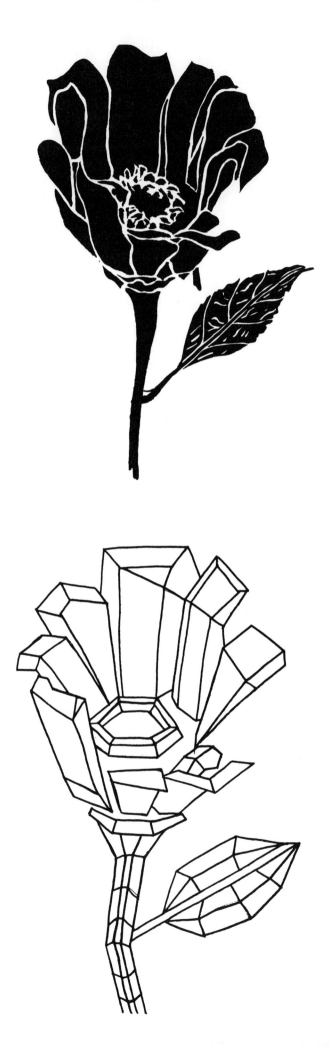

Four ways to look at a zinnia. Drawings by Martin
Ferris.